Cambridge Elements ☰

Elements in American Politics
edited by
Frances E. Lee
University of Maryland

CONTEMPORARY US POPULISM IN COMPARATIVE PERSPECTIVE

Kirk Hawkins
Brigham Young University, Utah

Levente Littvay
Central European University, Budapest

CAMBRIDGE
UNIVERSITY PRESS

CAMBRIDGE
UNIVERSITY PRESS

University Printing House, Cambridge CB2 8BS, United Kingdom

One Liberty Plaza, 20th Floor, New York, NY 10006, USA

477 Williamstown Road, Port Melbourne, VIC 3207, Australia

314–321, 3rd Floor, Plot 3, Splendor Forum, Jasola District Centre, New Delhi – 110025, India

79 Anson Road, #06–04/06, Singapore 079906

Cambridge University Press is part of the University of Cambridge.

It furthers the University's mission by disseminating knowledge in the pursuit of education, learning, and research at the highest international levels of excellence.

www.cambridge.org
Information on this title: www.cambridge.org/9781108456821
DOI: 10.1017/9781108644655

First published 2019

A catalogue record for this publication is available from the British Library.

ISBN 978-1-108-45682-1 Paperback
ISBN 978-1-108-64465-5 Online
ISSN 2515-1592 (print)
ISSN 2515-1606 (online)

Contemporary US Populism in Comparative Perspective

Elements in American Politics

DOI: 10.1017/9781108644655
First published online date: May 2019

Kirk Hawkins
Brigham Young University, Utah

Levente Littvay
Central European University, Budapest

Author for correspondence: Kirk Hawkins, kirk.hawkins@byu.edu, Levente Littvay, littvayl@ceu.edu

Abstract: With the victory of Donald Trump in the 2016 US presidential election, populists have come to power in the United States for the first time in many years. However, US political scientists have been flat-footed in their response, failing to anticipate or measure populism's impact on the campaign or to offer useful policy responses. In contrast, populism has long been an important topic of study for political scientists studying other regions, especially Latin America and Europe. The conceptual and theoretical insights of comparativist scholars can benefit Americanists, and applying their techniques can help US scholars and policymakers place events in perspective.

Keywords: populism, 2016 US election, democracy, public opinion, Trump

ISBNs: 9781108456821 (PB), 9781108644655 (OC)
ISSNs: 2515-1606 (online), 2515-1592 (print)

Contents

1 Introduction

"I love that. That's what I am," Trump said, "a popularist." He mangled the word. "No, no," Bannon said. "It's populist."
"Yeah, yeah," Trump insisted. "A popularist."

(Bob Woodward, *Fear: Trump in the White House*, 2018)

Scholars and pundits have been fascinated and troubled by the emergence of populism in the 2016 US presidential election. Almost from the moment Donald Trump entered the campaign, such commentators used the word "populist" pejoratively and often somewhat aimlessly to describe his antiestablishment rhetoric, his nativist and protectionist platform, and his ineloquent, boastful style (e.g., Latimer 2015; *The Telegraph 2015*; Williamson 2015). But as the quote above suggests, Trump's team was not scared to own the label. Perhaps just as noteworthy, several other candidates from the Republican Party employed a **populist**, as we define it, *Manichean people-versus-elite discourse* (Cillizza 2015; Phillips 2015). A major candidate in the Democratic Party, Bernie Sanders, built a movement using such a rhetoric in a more left-progressive platform, one that nearly won his party's nomination (Kazin 2016; Packer 2015).

The emergence of populism in the United States was troubling because it seemed to be part of a global wave threatening the institutions of liberal democracy (Diamond 2015; Foa and Mounk 2017; Galston 2018; Martinelli 2017; but see Mechkova, Lührmann, and Lindberg 2017). The rise to prominence of Trump and Sanders coincided with the near economic collapse of populist-led Greece and Venezuela and a populist campaign where the people of the United Kingdom voted to leave the European Union, the organization that was billed to provide stability and peace across Europe since World War II. What was previously seen as an affliction of developing countries was suddenly visible in elections across Europe and North America. In all of these countries, parties were emerging that claimed to defend the *will of ordinary citizens against a supposedly corrupt political class* that had sacrificed the good of the people for its selfish interests. Under some of these parties, aspects of democratic representation improved as participation increased, policy agendas shifted, and traditional parties became more aware of their distance from voters. But more often than not, populists concentrated government powers in the executive branch, tilted the electoral playing field, restricted civil liberties such as freedom of expression and the right of association, and polarized their populations – all in the name of the people.

With so much at stake, one can understand the incredible scholarly attention heaped on the study of populism after the US election. Several books were published to familiarize scholarly and popular audiences with the concept while explaining the Trump victory (Judis 2016; Muller 2016). Numerous special issues of journals appeared (Bornschier 2017; Dodd, Lamont, and Savage 2017; Engesser, Fawzi, and Larsson 2017; Hadiz and Chryssogelos 2017; Mudde and Rovira Kaltwasser 2018; Wodak and Krzyżanowski 2017).

But one important voice was missing from the conversation: Americanists. Scholars of American politics conducted many analyses of the campaign, but these focused on different explanations such as racial resentment, sexism, economic voting, authoritarian disposition, the quirks of the US primary system, or the electoral college (Hooghe and Dassonneville 2018; Jacobson 2017; Schaffner, Macwilliams, and Nteta 2018; Sides, Tesler, and Vavreck 2018a). A few mentioned the word "populism" as a casual descriptor, but none employed it as a systematically defined construct. Of over a hundred entries in the *Washington Post*'s Monkey Cage blog that analyzed the campaign, only a dozen mentioned populism as an important factor, and only one of these was written by an Americanist.[1]

Populism has long been ignored by American political science. The 2016 election is not the first time that populism has appeared in the United States, although it has been many decades since a putative populist has won the White House. Populists have appeared in the guise of third-party movements since at least the mid-nineteenth century (Bimes and Mulroy 2004). Indeed, US historians have provided excellent qualitative studies of earlier populist movements (Goodwyn 1976; Hofstadter 1960; Kazin 1998), and there is quantitative historical research on US populism coming from outside political science (Bonikowski and Gidron 2016). Yet, aside from work by Rahn and Oliver (Oliver and Rahn 2016; Rahn 2019) and a scattering of older articles (Axelrod 1967; Bimes and Mulroy 2004; Dryzek and Berejikian 1993; McClosky and Chong 1985), Americanists have not given serious attention to populism using their well-developed methodological apparatus (Rovira Kaltwasser et al. 2017). There has been almost no public opinion research, no topic analysis, and no experimental studies of populism in parties or in the electorate.

This contrasts entirely with the situation in Latin America and Europe. In these regions, populism has long been a topic of study for political scientists. The literature here dates back to the 1960s, with scholarly attention growing significantly over the past three decades. Conceptual debates initially prevented much in the way of quantitative, empirical research, but scholars studying these regions have increasingly refined their work through cross-regional

---

[1] Google search by the authors using the terms "monkey cage," "trump," and "populism" for 2015 through November 15, 2016, conducted in February 2018. One Monkey Cage post was written by an Americanist noted for her study of populism, but she did not use the word in her post (Cramer 2016b).

comparisons. This includes important conceptual and measurement efforts – to identify what populism is and where we find it – as well as the study of populism's causes and consequences. Out of this have coalesced a few dominant paradigms to the study of populism, including the ideational approach we build on in this Element.

Americanists' lack of familiarity not only has kept them from contributing to the scholarly and policy conversation but may have blinded them to explanations for what took place in 2016 and after. This oversight began in the primaries, which scholars argued that Trump could never win because he lacked the imprimatur of the party elite (an advantage for a populist candidate); ran through the general election, which so many analysts called for Hilary Clinton (populist attitudes were not included in any of the survey models); and continued into Trump's first two years in office, as commentators struggled to anticipate policy moves such as pulling out of the Paris climate agreement (Trump argued he was "elected to represent the citizens of Pittsburgh, not Paris"). By not analyzing Trump's discourse or populism's polarizing effects, Americanists missed a key explanatory variable. Indeed, many US political scientists walked right into a populist trap, reacting to Trump's anti-elite rhetoric with normatively tinged critiques rather than theoretically and empirically founded countermeasures.

Our goal is to bring systematic comparative research on populism into the study of US politics. We argue that comparativists' conceptual and theoretical insights can benefit Americanists, providing sharper tools for analyzing populism at home while placing events in perspective for US scholars and policymakers. Specifically, a comparative perspective can inform Americanists in three ways, which define the main sections of this Element. First, Section 2 provides *conceptual and descriptive tools* to help understand what populism is and how to measure it, especially at the elite level. Next, Section 3 explains the *causes of populism*, mainly in the sense of why and how people come to support populist parties and movements, while providing tools for measuring populist attitudes in the electorate. Section 4 specifies the *consequences of populism*, especially for democratic institutions, and sheds light on how these can be mitigated. Section 5 concludes by pointing to the research program that emerges if, instead of reinventing the wheel, we incorporate the ideational definition and broader comparative ideas of populism into the Americanist research tradition.

For data, we rely primarily on studies of the 2016 US presidential race. These include a textual analysis of major campaign speeches and debates and an online public opinion survey conducted during the primaries. We also update the textual analysis with new data from Trump's first year in office. But, to place the recent US experience in a temporal and cross-regional comparative perspective, we draw from two public opinion surveys – the 2008 and 2012 Cooperative Congressional Elections Study – and public opinion surveys from Europe and Latin America. Finally, we merge a large dataset on the populist discourse of chief executives, from across the globe and within the United States, with data on democratic performance.

Many of the techniques and theories we apply will be new to Americanists. This is certainly the case for our textual analysis, which draws on methods designed in other disciplines; inventories for measuring populist attitudes, which were refined outside the United States; and the basic concept of populist discourse, which comes from Europe and Latin America. But we emphasize that a "comparative perspective" means more than just taking concepts and methods from the study of other countries and applying them to the United States. It means comparing data from the United States with those from other countries, placing the US case into relief through a larger analysis across space and time. Specific instances of populism cannot be well understood in isolation. Populism comes in many flavors and emerges in response to different contexts; while these specifics matter for certain instances, including the United States in 2016, we cannot distinguish the specific from the general unless we bring instances of populism together.

2 The Concept of Populism: Putting Leaders in Context

We start with a basic question: How populist is Donald Trump? Trump was not the only populist candidate in 2016, but because he was an early frontrunner and won the general election, he garnered most of the attention. Commentators were somewhat divided over his populism since the moment he first announced his candidacy. Many argued that he was a strong example of populism and that his election was part of a larger wave overtaking the West, threating liberal democracy (Calamur 2016; Carroll 2016; Grillo 2016; Inglehart and Norris 2016). Others were more hesitant, arguing that he lacked key components of the populist message, even if he had ideological affinities with other populists (Barr 2016; Mudde 2015). This was the case especially early in his admittedly self-centered campaign, which lacked emphasis on the virtues of the common people. Since coming to power, opinions also have varied, although a common view of Trump is that he betrayed his initially populist message by championing policies such as deregulation and tax cuts that benefited the rich (Heer 2016; Illing 2017).

Let us answer this question with data taken not from the campaign but – because we think the comparison is impressive – from Trump's first year in office. Figure 1 compares the level of populism in a sample of his first-year speeches to similar samples from other contemporary world leaders, both

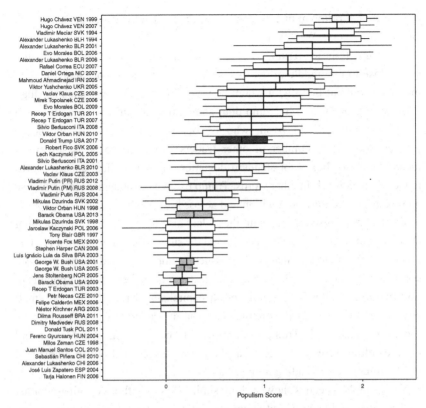

Populism Score

Figure 1 Populism scores based on speeches given by heads of governments (scale 0–2). This box-and-whisker plot shows the mean level of populism, along with a one-standard deviation of responses around that mean (box) and the 95 percent confidence interval around the mean (whiskers).

Note: A careful observer may wonder about these hard zeroes in the figure. The coding scheme asked for scores of 0, 1, or 2 for every speech. The hard zeroes scored 0 on all speeches. A later coding scheme, used only for the US presidents, allowed for in-between values. Coders were given the same anchors but allowed to use the full range of scores. We tested the US presidents both with this more refined method and by rounding the values (emulating a forced choice between 0, 1, and 2 for the coders). This change in methodology does not bias the results in any way, although the new approach offers higher intercoder reliability (when tested on a broader dataset) and narrower confidence intervals. Differences in the US presidential positions are minimal. For example, Trump moves down one place when the scores are rounded (though, admittedly, that one place is a four-way tie). Certainly, any deviations due to this updated methodology are statistically insignificant.

presidents and prime ministers, as well as a few recent US presidents (Barack Obama and George W. Bush).

As Figure 1 shows, Trump is clearly but only moderately populist, with a score close to the middle of the 0–2 scale. A few leaders score much higher, including some of those with whom he was initially compared, such as Hugo Chávez in Venezuela. Yet Trump does show up as populist – certainly much more than Obama and Bush, who lie on the bottom end of the scale. Furthermore, like a number of other leaders in this range he is somewhat inconsistent (see boxes for standard deviation). His individual speech scores ranged from 0 to 1.4. In other words, Trump received a moderate score because he is somewhat erratic both within and across his speeches.[2]

The technique used to generate these data also allows us to say something about the content of Trump's speeches and the substance of his populism (when it is present). Obviously, many of the issues Trump raises and the positions he takes are not shared by other leaders at the same or higher levels of populism. For example, while Trump believes in capitalism, deregulation, and small government, Chávez tried to implement what he called "twenty-first century socialism." And while Trump has promised to build a wall with Mexico and more carefully screen seekers of asylum, Chávez reached out to ethnic and gender minorities, including immigrants.

Yet Trump's speeches show striking similarities with those of other populist leaders. Just as Trump talked about "the corrupt politicians and their special interests [that] have rolled over this country" and his belief that "[t]oday the American working class is going to strike back" (words from his closing campaign speech), Chávez said that "you people, you are the giant that has awakened" and talked of their impending election victory over the scheming oligarchs that had "enslaved Venezuela and cast out the people" (2006 closing campaign speech). Likewise, Viktor Orbán of Hungary, in a 2010 campaign speech that marked his party's return to government, declared: "It will be decided whether there will be common national causes, for which we unite, or there remains the politics of individual interests, which doesn't care about people." Alexander Lukashenko, by then dictator of Belarus, proclaimed in his 2001 "reelection" campaign that "All these years we've gone through life with you – the people," while promising that "[c]riminals [the opposition] will never break into power." And Rafael Correa, about to become president of

---

[2] The narrower confidence interval around the estimates of US presidents is due to the coding differences discussed in the previous footnote. Trump's score is actually based on twice as many speeches as the other leaders, though this does not lead to a diminished variance or confidence interval due to Trump's relative inconsistency. This is also visible in Figure 2 where the speeches from the campaign are presented.

Ecuador, railed in his 2006 campaign against "the mafias connected to the political parties" and promised to create a "participatory democracy where the common citizen, the ordinary citizen has voice and vote."[3]

Definition

So where did we get this data, and why didn't US commentators have access to something like it back in 2016? The answer is that they did, but they had to look outside the United States at the work of comparativists. Over the past two decades, these political scientists have made considerable advances in terms of defining and measuring populism.

Until roughly a decade ago, comparativists struggled to study populism because they argued over what type of thing it was. Like the proverbial blind men studying the elephant, individual scholars focused on the characteristics of the movements they knew best, or on the features closest to their scholarly subfields. In Latin America, where much of the earliest work was done starting in the 1960s, definitions initially drew from a sociological perspective that identified populism as a type of multiclass coalition held together by statist economic development policies and an anti-status-quo ideology. These were common attributes of then-recent populist movements, such as those of Juan Domingo Perón and his wife Evita in Argentina, or Getúlio Vargas in Brazil (Cardoso and Faletto 1979; Di Tella 1965; Germani 1978; Ianni 1975; Weffort 1978). A decade or two later, scholarship shifted slightly, drawing from an economic approach defining populism as short-sighted macroeconomic policy-making designed to please the masses. These were features of governments in Mexico, Peru, and Argentina that responded to the region's debt crisis in the 1980s with inflationary economic policies (Dornbusch and Edwards 1991; Sachs 1989).

However, scholars began to question these definitions when newer waves of populism appeared in the 1990s promoting market-oriented economic reforms, especially in Latin America. These leaders and their movements framed the effort to privatize state-owned enterprises and deregulate the economy using the same pro-people, anti-elite message as earlier statist movements (Roberts 1995; Weyland 1999). Thus, they sounded or felt like earlier populists, even if their policies were different. At about this time, a new wave of radical right parties appeared in Western Europe that showed equally striking similarities with earlier populist movements from Latin

---

[3] Quotes here come from campaign speeches used to derive the scores in Figure 1. Original texts are available at https://populism.byu.edu/Pages/Data under US 2016 Presidential Campaign Speeches.

America and the United States. While European parties adopted very different policy positions around a nativist, anti-EU message, they used a similar pro-people, anti-elitist rhetoric (Mudde 2004).

These similarities in rhetoric have led a growing number of political theorists and comparativists to define populism in terms of a minimal set of ideas, rather than any particular set of policies or coalitions (Canovan 1981; de la Torre 2000; Laclau 1977). This ideational approach defines populism as a political discourse or "thin-centered ideology," one that frames democracy as a struggle between the will of the common people and a conspiring elite.

Although there are various ways of slicing up populism in the ideational approach (cf. Hawkins 2009; Mudde 2007), it generally includes two key elements. First is the notion of people-centrism, or the belief that politics should be the expression of a reified will of the common people, who are romanticized and seen as the embodiment of democratic virtue. Who "the people" are can vary. Left populists adopt a so-called inclusionary definition that explicitly courts ethnic minorities and more vulnerable groups; right-wing populists follow an "exclusionary" pattern that tries to restrict the people to previously dominant groups (Mudde and Rovira Kaltwasser 2013a). But populism circumscribes the demos by ascribing greater legitimacy to the opinions of "ordinary" citizens, and it essentializes this popular will, setting it up as the ultimate political standard and something that is "out there," knowable by those in tune with this democratic spirit.

Second is anti-elitism, or the view that political representatives and their powerful allies have become corrupt and are knowingly pursing their selfish interests at the expense of the people. Populism has a Manichaean cosmology that sees the side of good (the will of the people) arrayed against a knowing, agential evil – in this case, the elite (Dryzek and Berejikian 1993). As with the people, the elite's identity is a function of the populist's ideology. For many left populists it is an economic elite constituted by wealthy business owners, while for right populists it is a cultural and political class constituted by the traditional politicians and their intellectual allies. Either way, populists demonize this group and see it in conspiratorial terms, as a unitary actor that is working consciously against the righteous will of the people for its selfish interests.

From these core elements flow corollary attributes. Because populists believe the democratic system has been subverted, they call for systematic, institutional change rather than ordinary, piecemeal reform; they take an "anything goes" attitude toward liberal norms such as the rights of people holding opposing views; and they may attack evidence-based reasoning, because the elite presumably exploit these to protect and justify their corrupt rule (Hawkins 2009).

Democratic theorists see some of these attributes as positive because they serve to bring about institutional change and to include previously excluded groups (Canovan 1999). But these attributes also work against liberal democratic institutions that are designed to serve as checks on tyranny (Abts and Rummens 2007; Canovan 1999; Urbinati 1998).

An important part of the ideational approach is the observation that populism represents a unique type of ideas. Populism scholars suggest a variety of terms for capturing its qualities, such as "discursive frame," "style," or "thin-centered ideology," but the gist is that populism differs from traditional ideologies such as liberalism, conservatism, or socialism, because it is not consciously articulated and provides relatively few policy prescriptions. Rather, it is closer to a personality characteristic or a frame (Aslanidis 2016; Hawkins and Rovira Kaltwasser 2017; Moffitt 2016). This ontological status has implications for how populism should be measured and theorized (which we describe later), but it also clarifies two conceptual concerns for comparativists. One of these is the question of what other "isms" are out there besides populism. Populism scholars have in fact identified other political discourses, all of which can be distinguished from populism by their cosmology (Manichaean or universalist) and their notion of who the important political actors are (people, citizens, state, nation, etc.). Among these are pluralism, which shares populism's democratic underpinnings but opts for a universalistic cosmology that accepts differences of opinion as inevitable and avoids labeling opponents as enemies, and elitism or technocracy, which adopts populism's Manichaean outlook but reverses the normative positions of the people and the elite (Caramani 2017; Mudde 2004; Ochoa Espejo 2011; Plattner 2010).

Seeing populism as a distinct type of idea also makes it easier to explain the historical presence of populists on the left and the right. Because populism is not as consciously articulated and provides relatively few policy prescriptions, it has to be attached to other "host ideologies" that can fill it out with specific issue positions (Freeden 2017; Mudde and Rovira Kaltwasser 2013b). Hence, populism can be found anywhere along traditional ideological spectra, and ideological labels such as "left" and "right" should be used to define subtypes of populism, rather than populism per se. It is also important not to confuse ideologically driven policy positions (such as anti-immigration or anti-corporate sentiments) with populism itself. The real question is not whether left or right versions of populism are truer, but why these and other versions appear at particular historical moments and what their consequences are for democracy.

To be clear, not every comparativist endorses this minimal ideational definition, and at least two other perspectives are prominent. One is a *political strategic* one that accepts the centrality of populist ideas but either mistrusts the sincerity and importance of these ideas for political behavior or prefers to apply the term to certain kinds of organization, especially those with charismatic leadership and a movement structure (Weyland 2001; R. R. Barr 2009). The other is often called the *Essex School* for its founder, Ernesto Laclau (2005), a political theorist at the eponymous university. Rooted in cultural critiques of Marxism, this approach sees populist discourse as a strategy for building a politically viable working-class identity and thus limits instances of populism to larger movements of the left.

The ideational approach differs from these other perspectives in important ways. It argues that we should not limit populism to specific organizational forms but should treat these forms as variables to be analyzed; likewise, it claims that populism's relationship to democracy is often problematic, and that pluralist discourses may be better facilitators of democratic transitions. However, it unites with these other approaches in affirming that a party or movement must use the same kind of people versus elite rhetoric in order to be considered populist and that we should be careful about limiting populism to any particular historical period or set of issue positions. Whatever their precise causal impact, populist ideas are specific, measurable, and definitional.

Measurement

One of the most important features of the ideational approach is its effort at measuring populism by analyzing populist ideas. In earlier decades, scholars made few attempts to build datasets of populist leaders, although some edited volumes implied that it was possible to categorize leaders or governments (Conniff 1999; Dornbusch and Edwards 1991). When the first datasets appeared, they were an important advance that facilitated comparative analysis (Kitschelt 1997; Mudde 2007; van Kessel 2015). But decisions about who was populist still relied on qualitative, expert judgments that were difficult to replicate, and all of these were dichotomous measures that discarded information. Few of these measures distinguished populist ideas from organizational features, making it difficult to determine which of these elements was responsible for populism's effects on democratic institutions (Doyle 2011; Kenny 2017).

The new focus on populism's ideational content meant that it was possible to develop techniques for measuring these ideas at both the level of the political elites and the level of citizens. At the level of elites, where the work of measuring populist ideas started, populism was mostly gauged through content analysis of speeches or other party documents. The earliest textual analyses focused on individual politicians or parties in single countries

(Armony and Armony 2005; Jagers and Walgrave 2007), but comparativists soon began measuring the populist discourse of multiple parties and politicians across countries and across time (Hawkins 2009; Rooduijn and Pauwels 2011; Bonikowski and Gidron 2016). Their studies showed that populist ideas consistently characterized most of the politicians who were historically considered populist. This finding confirmed the conceptual significance of these ideas while showing it was possible to approach the study of populist discourse systematically. Often, quantitative measures were paired with qualitative analyses that could fill out the rich content of different leaders' discourses. Who are the people? Who is the elite? And how do these identities shift across campaigns, terms in office, or status in opposition and government?

To better grapple with the latent, diffuse elements of populist rhetoric, most content analyses were human coded or semiautomated. Human coders could pick up quickly on ideas that were expressed with whole phrases (for example, not just "people" but "the people") or with different phrases having similar meanings (such as "working Americans" and "the American people"); above all, they could determine the meaning of otherwise identical words (for instance, whether "the people" references the romanticized few or everyone in the country). In contrast, efforts to apply fully automated techniques were elusive. Several dictionary-based measures appeared (Bonikowski and Gidron 2016; Dai and Shao 2016; Jagers and Walgrave 2007; Rooduijn and Pauwels 2011), but these tended to work better with smaller numbers of countries where less translation of coding instruments was required. Supervised machine learning techniques were also attempted for specialized genres of text, such as party platforms, but it was difficult to make these work across multiple genres, and the corpus of training texts required for these analyses was usually too small to permit precise measures (Dai 2018; Hawkins and Silva 2019).

At the level of citizens, scholars using the ideational approach expended an enormous effort to measure populist attitudes in public opinion surveys. The goal was the creation of an item inventory that could work across multiple countries, facilitating cross-regional research. While several inventories were proposed (Akkerman, Mudde, and Zaslove 2014; Cooperative Study of Electoral Systems 2016; Schulz et al. 2018; Castanho Silva et al. 2019), all of them took the same approach, presenting survey respondents with populist-sounding phrases (or non-populist ones) and gauging their level of (dis)agreement – a tacit recognition that what was being measured were latent ideas, not manifest ones like traditional ideologies and issue positions. Although some initial work was actually done in the United States (Hawkins, Riding, and Mudde 2012), most of the new datasets covered

Europe and Latin America, where a significant body of data quickly accumulated. Strikingly, most surveys had similar findings, showing that populist attitudes existed at the level of citizens as a bundle of ideas that were relatively stable and widespread across countries, and that these attitudes varied in predictable ways with individual-level attributes such as education, age, and gender. These attitudes were remarkably strong across all countries where they were measured, suggesting that populist attitudes are common. Just as important, these attitudes correlated with voting intention and vote choice for parties known for their populism (Akkerman, Mudde, and Zaslove 2014; Hawkins, Riding, and Mudde 2012; Elchardus and Spruyt 2016; S. Van Hauwaert and van Kessel 2018).

Although these methods became standard (textual analysis for political elites, surveys for citizens), comparativists continued experimenting with new measures, often by taking techniques designed for one level and applying them to another. For example, while textual analysis of citizens' language was difficult given the lack of a consistent corpus of texts in most settings, the technique was used in isolated studies such as fieldwork or experiments, where it could extract data from open-ended questions and semi-structured interviews (Abts, Kochuyt, and van Kessel 2019; Busby, Gubler, and Hawkins 2019). Comparativists also applied survey techniques to the study of elites (politicians) by using modified versions of populist attitude inventories (Andreadis and Ruth 2019). This technique made it possible to match populist attitudes of citizens with their political representatives, helping scholars measure ideational congruence. Finally, comparativists developed expert surveys that could measure populist discourse among party leaders. These were especially promising ways of comparing populism with parties' traditional issue positions and ideologies (Polk et al. 2017; Wiesehomeier 2019).

Trump and the 2016 Presidential Election

Very little of this work made it into the publications of Americanists, or even US journalists, during or after the 2016 presidential election. The earliest efforts were instead by comparativists or US scholars from outside political science (cf. Lamont, Park, and Ayala-Hurtado 2017). Our own work was one of these early attempts (Hawkins 2016a; Hawkins and Kaltwasser 2018). During the election campaign, we measured the level of populist discourse in speeches and debate transcripts by all of the major candidates, and for this Element we conducted a second analysis of Trump's speeches while in office (as glimpsed in Figure 1). For both analyses we used a technique called holistic grading, a type of textual analysis from educational psychology used for grading student essays (White 1985). It works well across countries with different languages, and has high levels of reliability with relatively small numbers of texts (Sudweeks, Reeve, and Bradshaw 2004). It assigns a numerical value to a text based on the content, but unlike traditional content analysis that works at the level of words or sentences, it requires coders to read each text in its entirety and assign a single score, based on a grading (coding) rubric and a set of anchor texts illustrating each point in an interval-level scale. The scale we used was based on previous work and has three values: 0 (no populism), 1 (clear populists elements, but used inconsistently or with a mild tone), and 2 (clear populist elements used consistently and with a strong tone) (Hawkins, 2009). Just to be clear, by "populist elements" we mean the two core elements of populist discourse: a reified will of the common people and an evil, conspiring elite. Thus, we did not consider texts populist just because they were highly antagonistic or because they praised ordinary people. They had to situate the common people in a struggle with the establishment.

For the 2016 campaign, our sample included roughly two speeches per month for each candidate, with a focus on longer or more widely publicized speeches; we also included all of the debates during the general election campaign. A total of fifty-one texts were coded (two platforms, three debates – twice each – and forty-six speeches) yielding fifty-four candidate observations.

We also wanted to know what had happened with Trump's discourse after the election. For his first year in office, we coded a quota sample comparable to those we have coded for political chief executives (presidents and prime ministers) in other countries. This sample consists of four types of chief executive speeches: campaign, ribbon-cutting, international, and famous. Criteria for selecting the speeches can be found in the online appendix at the Team Populism website, https://populism.byu.edu/, but the underlying logic is to include speeches that are more likely to feature populism (campaign and famous speeches) and others that are less likely (international and especially ribbon-cutting). The scores are averaged together with all texts weighted equally. The main difference between the Trump analysis and those performed on other chief executives is that we doubled the size of the sample, with two speeches per category instead of one, for a total of eight.

For both analyses, the campaign and Trump's first year, two coders read each text, assigned a score, and provided a short, written justification for their score with illustrative quotes, all of which were recorded in a coding rubric. In these analyses, coders also provided a decimal score, and they provided sub-scores for the key elements of populist discourse (reified people and conspiring elite). These sub-scores were a new feature giving added information on some of the

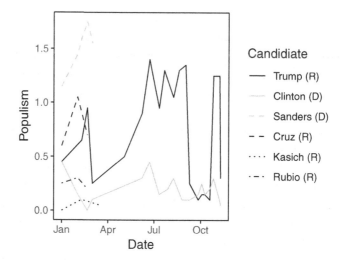

Figure 2 Populism scores based on speeches or debates during the campaign (scale 0–2).

candidates. All of the coding rubrics, scores, and original texts are available at the Team Populism website.[4]

Let us first consider results for the campaign. Figure 2 arrays all of the US candidates' scores (speeches and debates) chronologically, with announcement speeches set as a common starting point. The trend lines draw attention to the stability (or, in the case of Trump, the instability) of the candidates' discourses, but let us first say something about the candidates' average levels, where there are also obvious differences. If we calculate an unweighted average of all the texts (speeches and debates), Sanders is the most populist of all the candidates (mean = 1.5), followed by Ted Cruz and Trump (both at 0.8). The rest score low. Most of these results confirm the less systematic judgments of the pundits: Sanders, Trump, and Cruz are more populist than Clinton, Kasich, and Rubio. One result that may be surprising is the substantially higher score for Sanders.

Partly because of the result for Sanders, critics may wonder just how high these scores are in comparative perspective, and whether the technique incorporates bias toward the ideological left. Regarding bias, we simply note that

---

[4] Intercoder reliability for the campaign texts was Krippendorff's alpha = 0.69, a moderate level of reliability. Intercoder reliability for Trump's presidential speeches cannot be calculated using standard metrics because only five of eight texts were coded jointly, but for these the coders never differ by more than 0.5 on the 0–2 scale, with an average difference of 0.2.

some of Trump's scores are in the same range as Sanders, and that his low average is the product of high variability. As for comparative perspective, our earlier data on chief executives provides some help: we know several leaders score much higher than Trump in office, and that as president he scores roughly in the middle of the scale – about where he is in the campaign. Furthermore, closer analysis of the campaign speech scores shows that other countries are sometimes higher than the US in 2016 (Hawkins 2009). Sanders in particular is still below the most noted left-wing populists of Latin America, though hardly in good company around Yushchenko and Ahmadinejad.

Of course, the point in creating a time series for the US campaign is not just to take a more accurate sounding of the candidates but to see if there are any trends or movements that tell us more about their populism. What stands out for most of the candidates is the stability of their discourse: Clinton never goes above 0.5, for example, while Sanders never drops below 1.5. Whether this is a sign of their sincerity or their ability to stay on message, their rhetoric is fairly predictable. In contrast, Trump's discourse stands out for its inconsistency. He appears to become more populist across the course of his campaign, especially after May 2016 when he changes his campaign team and captures the nomination. Even then, his scores dropped noticeably during key moments, especially the presidential debates and his victory speech.

We think the inconsistency of Trump's populist discourse is as important as the average level. Closer analysis of this inconsistency reveals a great deal about his likely *sincerity,* and we think the picture here partially – but not entirely – confirms the suspicions of his critics who see his populism as incomplete or insincere. Our educated guess is that variability in Trump's populism is the product of his speechwriters. The fact that his debate scores are so low, and that his scores trended more upward after he adopted a new campaign team in May 2016, suggests that Trump himself is not all that populist, and hence receives low scores when speaking extemporaneously. When Trump gives prepared remarks, his speechwriters help fill in the gaps of his populist discourse, and he receives higher scores.

To test this hypothesis, we went back and identified which of Trump's speeches and debates were given with a teleprompter and which ones were given without; while a teleprompter doesn't guarantee that Trump was following a script, the lack of a teleprompter means that he was forced to speak extemporaneously. We then measured several linguistic markers that could distinguish Trump's prepared speeches from extemporaneous ones. Specifically, we measured the average length of words, the average length of sentences, and the frequency of one of his pet words: "great." We also compared the level of populism in the two groups of speeches, with and without teleprompter. The hypothesis is that Trump's prepared speeches should have longer words and sentences, make less frequent use of pet words, and express stronger populism.[5]

As the results in Figure 3 demonstrate (once again, the box-and-whisker plot shows the mean level of each indicator, with the standard deviation in the box and the 95 percent confidence interval in the whiskers), there is a dramatic difference in linguistic markers and the level of populism depending on whether the speech was given with or without a teleprompter. Trump's speeches with teleprompters all have longer words, longer sentences, less frequent use of his pet words, and higher levels of populism. This is powerful evidence that Trump's populism is not entirely his own.

This does not mean we should write off Trump as an insincere populist. The more accurate label is a "half-populist." Trump has key elements of populism even in his extemporaneous speeches, and they are strong. Specifically, while his extemporaneous speeches are often missing people-centric references, anti-elite messages are present throughout. To assess this quantitatively, we drew from the sub-scores that our coders generated at the time they coded his speeches for overall populism. We asked them to independently score two elements, people-centrism and anti-elitism, on the same 0–2 scale used for the overall populism score. This effort was a new initiative, and we were uncertain how the measures would perform – the more specific the idea being measured, the less suited holistic grading techniques are. This is why we used traditional content-analytical techniques to measure the linguistic elements of his speeches and debates. In fact, intercoder reliability here was moderate for people-centrism (Krippendorff's alpha = 0.67) but quite low for anti-elitism (0.25). Given the large number of texts coded, we decided to consider the results anyway, knowing that higher levels of error would yield more conservative estimates of any difference in means.

The results in Figure 4 show that both elements – people-centrism and anti-elitism – were higher in Trump's speeches and debates with a teleprompter than in the ones without a teleprompter. But while the increase in people-centrism is large and statistically significant, the increase for anti-elitism is much smaller and statistically insignificant. Essentially, Trump's speechwriters brought his people-centrism up to the level of his anti-elitism. Thus, unlike other elements of populism, Trump seems to have always had an antiestablishment rhetoric. Indeed, both in the coders' debriefings with us and in the comments and quotes in their coding rubrics it

---

[5] We used Microsoft Word's File Properties Statistics to count word and sentence length, without spaces included, and the word search function to look for pet words. The coders viewed each speech and debate using YouTube to look for a teleprompter. We double-checked the coding for 10 percent of the speeches and found 100 percent agreement on all new indicators.

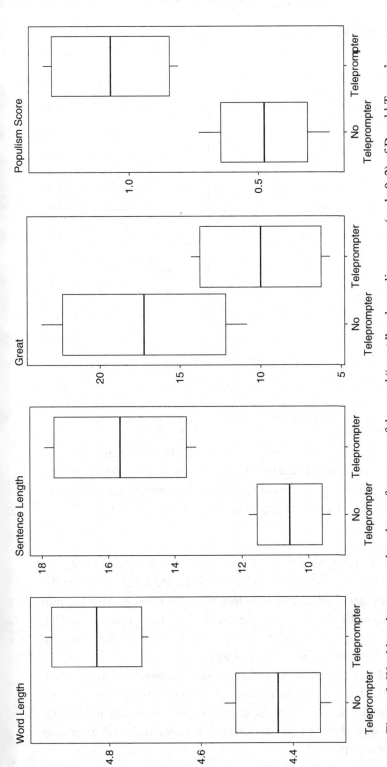

Figure 3 Word length, sentence length, use frequency of the word "great," and populism score (scale 0–2) of Donald Trump's speeches on and off a teleprompter. The box-and-whisker plot shows the mean level, along with a one-standard deviation of responses around that mean (box), and the 95 percent confidence interval (whiskers).

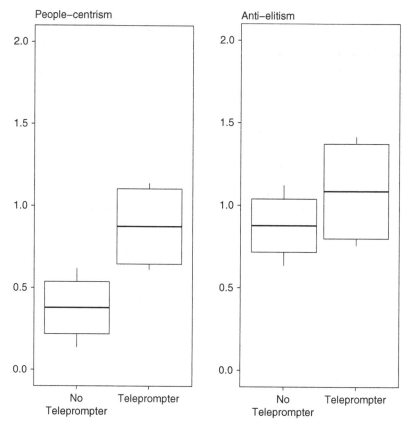

Figure 4 People-centrism and anti-elitism scores of Donald Trump's speeches on and off a teleprompter (scale 0–2). The box-and-whisker plot shows the mean level along with a one-standard deviation of responses around that mean (box), and the 95 percent confidence interval (whiskers).

was clear that Trump tended to criticize elites – Washington, liberals, the global financial establishment – in all his texts. However, in his earlier speeches they observed that he was less likely to mention the American people or describe them as the protagonists of their political system. Instead, Trump tended to refer to himself and his team as the ones who would save America and make it great again.

Note that this is a clear contrast with the more consistent rhetoric of Sanders, which earned him a higher populism score. Data points for the five speeches we scored are too few to try splitting the sample, but his component averages for people-centrism and anti-elitism are 1.5 and 1.6, respectively, and never drop below 0.8 for any speech.

What about Trump's first-year speeches? We stole most of our own thunder by presenting the results in Figure 1, which show Trump in comparison with other national leaders during their terms in office, and where we found that he was roughly in the middle of the pack in the close company of Hungary's Orbán, Italy's Silvio Berlusconi, Czech Republic's Robert Fico, and Poland's Lech Kaczynski of the mid- to late 2000s. The overall level of populism in Trump's speeches has remained essentially unchanged – somewhere around 0.7–0.8 in the campaign and in office (bearing in mind that these averages are over mostly different samples). This itself is an important finding, because the level of populism for many leaders decreases after their campaigns, sometimes dramatically; Trump's populism has not declined. Perhaps just as important, the level of variability in his discourse has remained high (sd = 0.51; in the campaign speeches it was 0.50). Clearly, the variation in his first year cannot have the same cause as in the campaign – all of these speeches rely on a teleprompter, and so his remarks are probably all scripted. What else could be the cause? This is necessarily more speculative, because we do not know who wrote each speech, but it may reflect a volatile pick of speechwriters and advisors. Trump's principal speechwriter from the campaign, Stephen Miller, remained an advisor and was well known for his right-populist outlook, but Steve Bannon, another right populist, fell out of favor and left the administration in August 2017; other advisors with a less populist bent, such as Trump's son-in-law Jared Kushner, have occasionally also had an influence on his speeches (*The Economist* 2017; Mascaro 2017). One way of testing this argument is to see whether the two elements of populism – people-centrism and anti-elitism – correlate with each other more within his speeches in office than they do among his speeches and debates from the campaign. We calculate this using Krippendorff's alpha and find that the agreement between people-centrism and anti-elitism in the campaign is only alpha=0.45, but in office it is alpha=0.84. Thus, when one element in his presidential speeches is missing, it is more likely that the other one is as well – evidence of populist and non-populist speechwriters, rather than the more complicated picture of Trump's own words.

Overall, we think it is still fair to say that Trump has only a partial affinity for populism born of a strong antiestablishment outlook and that this affinity grows depending on his choice of advisors. But at least in the campaign, Trump himself lacked a strong belief in the virtue of the *volonté générale* of the people. This may have implications for his impact on American democracy, which we discuss in the final section.

3 The Causes of Populism: Explaining the Victory *with Ethan Busby, Clemson University*

Conceptualizing and describing are important steps toward understanding populism, but as scholars we are also interested in its causes. Why does populism emerge in the 2016 election, or at earlier moments in US history? Do its causes mimic what we find in other countries? Furthermore, are these causes entirely structural, or is there an individual-level component in terms of the attributes of voters that support these populist forces? Finding answers to these questions does much more than satisfy our scientific curiosity; it can reshape our sense of what makes people vote and teach vital lessons to non-populist politicians, giving a sense of how to effectively confront and compete with populists.

Existing Explanations

Scholars of American politics have already offered a few basic explanations for Trump's victory and the recent rise of populist forces. Early on, some journalists and commentators suggested that Trump's support and the recent rise of populist movements were driven by the grievances of unskilled blue-collar laborers harmed by automation and the off-shoring of manufacturing and resource extraction industries. According to this economic argument, not only had government facilitated these trends through policies of free trade and unrestricted capital flows, but it combined these with regressive tax reforms and a shrinking social safety net that harmed the very workers hit hardest by globalization. While these were long-term trends, short-term factors such as the Great Recession aggravated these problems by leaving lower- and middle-class Americans indebted and jobless (all while the financial industry was being bailed out). Because these policies were championed by both parties – first Reagan/Bush I, then the Clinton Democrats, and again by Bush II – the "losers of globalization" turned to outsider candidates who preached against the system and promised a fairer world for the good people of America (Jacobson 2017; Johnston 2016; Sides and Tesler 2016).

A more common argument was that Trump's support was rooted in a clash over the spread of progressive values. Conservative Americans increasingly resented the push by progressive elites to transform traditional institutions of marriage and family and the religions that defended them. These concerns were often connected to feelings of anger over Civil Rights legislation and pro-immigration policies that seemed to benefit African-Americans or undocumented migrants at the expense of poorer white Americans. Americanists noted the very high correlation between racial resentment and anti-immigrant attitudes and the vote for Trump, who challenged the liberal elite with talk of Mexican "rapists" and a border wall that Mexico would pay for, or pointed to a nostalgic past with promises to select judges that would roll back progressive achievements (Sides, Tesler, and Vavreck 2018b). While some scholars saw these attitudes as a type of resentment toward the injustices of globalization and a lack of democratic voice (Cramer 2016a; Skocpol and Williamson 2013), others suggested that these views reflect lingering racism and authoritarian attitudes, a set of trait-like qualities that drive people to seek moral clarity and conformity to traditional values (Hooghe and Dassonneville 2018; Schaffner, Macwilliams, and Nteta 2018).

Finally, Americanists emphasized the unique set of institutions that prevented the success of previous movements in recent years, while facilitating Trump's victory. These included the combination of electoral rules for Electoral College votes – first-past-the-post, reinforcing a two-party system in presidential elections – and rules for nominating candidates. The first-past-the-post system erected a formidable obstacle to populists running as third-party or independent candidates, and many of the major third-party candidates of the past two centuries were populist (Kazin 1998). But a populist who captured the nomination of one of the two major parties would have a significant advantage in the general election, enjoying the support of voters who might not particularly like the candidate's qualities but still leaned partisan on key issues. And while party leaders' control over nominations could have prevented populist outsiders from running through the two traditional parties, the nomination rules had been liberalized since the 1970s as the dominance of the caucus system took a back seat to primaries, giving the voters more power to nominate. Primary voters tended to be the strongest party activists, and in recent decades, a gradual process of ideological sorting has meant that these were increasingly radical activists. Trump appeared at an ideal moment to capitalize on this radical partisan electorate and capture the nomination.

The Ideational Argument

Comparativists accept all of these theories as explaining important parts of populism. We cannot understand why voters support populist versions of left or right political actors without taking into account the issues that define them as left or right. And we cannot explain the emergence of populist actors without identifying the electoral rules and party system configurations that facilitate their efforts.[6] But a story that focuses only on issue positions or institutions is

---

[6] While some comparativists offer strong arguments in favor of particular causal mechanisms (Inglehart and Norris 2017), most take a broader approach emphasizing the combination of economic and cultural factors and institutional constraints. For a few examples focused on the populist radical right, see Betz (1994), Kitschelt (1997), or Mudde (2007). For a nice account emphasizing the role of institutions in the United Kingdom, see Carter (2005).

missing the fundamental question of why voters want a *populist* (Hawkins, Read, and Pauwels 2017; Mudde and Rovira Kaltwasser 2017). After all, a voter who is a loser from cultural globalization could support a non-populist version of an anti-immigrant, conservative party, while a loser from economic globalization could support a party offering an expanded welfare state and trade controls without any populist rationale. Something about populism itself is important for voters and politicians, important enough that they are drawn to it as a way of framing their issue positions.

To explain what drives support for populists, comparativists using the ideational approach have proposed an individual-level, psychological theory about populist ideas and their activation among voters (Hawkins and Rovira Kaltwasser 2019). This ideational theory takes issue positions and institutions into account but embeds them in a larger story about where populist ideas come from and how they are activated and mobilized.

The theory starts with the premise that voters for populist parties also have populist ideas in their heads; populism is not just a feature of political elites. Because these ideas may not be expressed, the literature refers to them as populist attitudes (Hawkins, Rovira Kaltwasser, and Andreadis 2018). Comparativists have devised a number of survey inventories for gauging these attitudes. Responses to these inventories cohere sensibly and correlate with other indicators such as voting, but they also show that populist attitudes are widespread across many countries at similar levels (Akkerman, Zaslove, and Spruyt 2017; Spruyt, Keppens, and Van Droogenbroek 2016; S. Van Hauwaert and van Kessel 2018). The fact that these attitudes are so widespread suggests that they are largely given, the product of personality and socialization in a democracy, rather than the result of short-term events. This finding supports the assertion of theorists who argue that populism is innate to a belief in democracy (Canovan 1999; Panizza 2005). Once citizens come to believe in themselves as the rightful bearers of sovereignty, they acquire the potential for identifying themselves as "the people" and their representatives as part of a powerful ruling class. Thus, the existence of populist attitudes is not likely to vary much across democracies, although it may vary within them as a result of personality (do you tend toward moral absolutes and to demonize your opponents?) and demographics (how has education, age, ethnicity, or religion shaped your understanding of how the political world works?).

The next step of the argument is to explain when populist attitudes become salient. The fact that people have a set of attitudes does not mean they automatically express them. Many other personality traits (Mondak et al. 2010), attitudes (Feldman 2003; Hetherington and Weiler 2009; McCann 2009;

Stenner 2005), and frames (Chong and Druckman 2007; Nelson, Oxley, and Clawson 1997) are moderated by external factors – they are dispositions that must be activated in order to be expressed. The same seems to be true with populist attitudes. After all, there are other political discourses that share some points with populism (such as pluralism's belief in popular sovereignty), and some people hold these beliefs simultaneously (Akkerman, Mudde, and Zaslove 2014).

Ideational scholars identify three broad factors that explain this activation of populist attitudes. The first is context. In order to be sensible, populism requires a context of actual failures of democratic representation that can be construed as intentional elite misconduct. In many countries this context is widespread, systematic corruption: the political system is basically set up as a competition over rents, rather than a competition over the production of public goods. Those on the losing side of this competition can rightly argue that their representatives are selling out the people for selfish interests. This may explain why populist forces are more successful in developing countries; these are places where corruption is deepest and most widespread (Hawkins 2010; Kenny 2017). But even in countries with highly programmatic party competition, politicians may find their policy options constrained by outside forces, or they may simply want to push an ideology they believe in, even though doing so ignores the interests and concerns of part of the electorate. Thus, in the words of Mair (2011), politicians' efforts to be "responsible" undermine their democratic imperative to be "responsive." Here too, voters may feel that politicians are violating democratic norms by denying citizens the right to an equal voice.

The second factor is the use of a populist frame by political entrepreneurs (Busby, Gubler, and Hawkins 2019). Even with some objective failure of democratic representation, voters can draw on multiple ways of interpreting their problem. While they may eventually see these problems in a populist light anyway, this process can be catalyzed by populist politicians employing populist rhetoric. This rhetoric has specific components. Failures of democratic representation must be seen as a challenge to a broader democratic subject – the people – and they must be attributed to the knowing actions of an elite. Thus, populist rhetoric must reference the right in- and out-groups while engaging in a particular kind of dispositional attribution (Hameleers, Bos, and de Vreese 2016).

Finally, to become fully mobilized, voters need an organizational vehicle that embodies their concerns. Would-be populist voters need an organization that coordinates their competing interests and gives them confidence in a successful effort, even as it satisfies their populist urge for direct involvement. Generally, three types of populist organization are common (Hawkins and Rovira Kaltwasser 2019; Mudde and Rovira Kaltwasser 2017). First, populists can organize as an institutionalized political party, a common option in politics already characterized by programmatic party competition, where traditional issue divides are still salient and where politicians and citizens are accustomed to parties with clear programs and permanent, professionalized organizations. This strategy is most effective when the barriers to entry for new political parties are low. Second, they can organize as a charismatic movement. This is more common in developing countries, where programmatic divides are relatively weak and where the high demand for populism makes it possible to sustain large, heterogeneous movements of supporters; indeed, charismatic leadership may be the only feasible way of organizing such a diverse set of interests. Though certainly not a case of a developing country, Donald Trump probably falls into this category. Finally, populists can organize as a grassroots movement, one that retains a nonhierarchical network of activists but depends on spontaneous coordination rather than charismatic leadership to sustain its efforts. This type exists in many countries, although the lack of leadership means that it tends to lose elections and remain on the political margins, and thus is rarely tracked by political scientists. Of course, the grassroots nature of the organizational structure does not rule out facilitating infrastructural, financial, or logistical support from above when the base's interests align with those of other political actors. Instances of these movements are visible in contemporary US politics, including both the Tea Party and Occupy Wall Street.[7]

Explaining the US Campaign: Country-Level Predictors

In terms of country-level predictions, the ideational theory is largely compatible with existing explanations by Americanists for the emergence of populism in the 2016 US presidential election, although it offers some clarifying insights.

To begin with, the ideational theory accepts the role of institutional opportunities created by the combination of two-party system and open nomination system, but with the caveat that institutional barriers to entry are generally more significant when the demand for populism is modest, as in much of contemporary Western Europe. In countries where demand for populists is quite high, as in much of Latin America, rules can be hastily rewritten or reinterpreted to allow favored populist politicians to run; indeed, whole constitutions are written and rewritten once radical populists are in office. Even in established democracies,

---

[7] For an extensive discussion of the hybrid nature of such grassroots movements, see Skocpol and Williamson (2013).

formal institutions may not be as strong as we think when populations become angry (Levitsky and Ziblatt 2018). Thus, in a context of greater representational failure, constraints on the effective number of parties and rules about nominations and primaries may not be an obstacle to populism. This would mean that first-past-the-post electoral rules slowed the progress of populists in the United States for over a century because the demand for populism was only felt by a minority of the electorate.

Furthermore, the ideational theory points out an additional institutional constraint in the need for an effective organization that combines the very different interests of a large populist coalition. In the case of Trump, access to the Republican Party apparatus was a significant resource once he got to the general election, and after the election it could ensure a governing majority in Congress. But there and in the primaries, another important organizational dimension was his qualities as a leader. His fame as a successful businessman and television personality, his boastfulness, and his skillful use of media were crucial for presenting would-be supporters with an outsider candidate who could credibly embody the collective will of ordinary people and clean up government if he were elected.

The ideational theory also accepts country-level factors emphasized by Americanists, namely, the impact of economic and cultural change in creating new sets of grievances among voters. But it adds two clarifications. First, voter grievances were not just about unsatisfied material needs or opposition to progressive values, but a belief that these changes were the result of intentional political neglect and the selfish machinations of those who were elected to be their representatives. This kind of voter demand was more specific and severe than the issue positions or left-right ideology measured in traditional surveys and would not be fully captured by these measures. The next section explores the individual-level evidence for this claim.

Second, while the sense of grievance was real and connected to reality for an important subset of voters, the objective conditions for these grievances were weaker than in other countries, and the resulting populist manifestations were relatively moderate. Trump was elected in a country where corruption was low and the economy was doing well. According to Transparency International's Corruption Perceptions Index (a composite measure of corruption based on a variety of business surveys), in 2016 the United States was ranked eighteenth best out of 176 countries across the world (Transparency International n.d.). This is nowhere near the levels one finds in countries with strong populists in power (Hawkins 2010; Castanho Silva 2019). While the government deficit was clearly enormous, the economy had improved significantly following the Great Recession, with unemployment levels of under

5 percent, positive annual GDP growth rates (since 2010), and an over 3 percent increase in wages (Federal Reserve Bank of Atlanta n.d.; US Department of Labor n.d.; The World Bank n.d.).

Again, the distribution of these positive tendencies did not mean everyone benefitted equally. Many lower-class people achieved poorer personal outcomes than these numbers would suggest or, despite the growth, were still struggling to recover a standard of living they enjoyed before 2008. As Oliver and Rahn (2016) and Rahn (2019) have shown, there was a sense of failed representation among a segment of the electorate that felt left behind by economic globalization and betrayed by secular progressivism, and this sense of failed representation was linked to populist attitudes and voting.

However, as we have tried to make clear with our careful assessment of Trump's discourse as well as that of the other candidates, the United States was not experiencing extremely high levels of populism. Whatever critics may think of Trump's moral failings and leadership skills (problems in their own right), his discourse and that of most other candidates were only moderately populist in absolute terms. While some voters felt enough resentment to fuel a populist uprising, these feelings were not widespread enough to make Americans abandon the Constitution or call for a complete end to the traditional party system. Thus, in comparative perspective, the United States in 2016 was an instance of populist forces similar to ones we often see in wealthy democracies, where failures of responsible partisan governance generate modest (and occasionally successful) populist movements for not-quite-revolutionary change. As we will show later, this still leaves real cause for concern for US democracy, but it puts the election in a bit more perspective.

Populist Attitudes and Their Correlates in the United States

The ideational approach goes beyond these aggregate-level predictions to offer additional, unique expectations at the individual level. Here the argument is that populist attitudes are common among US voters, similar to the high levels we find in other countries, with more variation inside the country than across. Average levels of populist attitudes stay fairly constant, and their correlations with predictors such as age, gender, or education should be relatively stable. What matters is whether these attitudes are active. In the United States in 2016, where there was some potential demand and where populist candidates were available to offer the supply catalyzing that demand, we should find a modest subset of voters whose attitudes are in fact associated with their vote choice.

To test the first of these individual-level expectations, concerning the existence of these attitudes and their stability, we start with a little comparative data on populist attitudes in the United States at three recent moments – the 2008,

2012, and 2016 presidential elections – and juxtapose these with recent samples from Europe and Latin America. This allows us to compare countries with prominent right- and left-wing populists, highlighting the lack of variation of populist attitudes across multiple regional contexts. We then look more closely inside the United States by showing the stability of populist attitudes across time, first by examining the average levels of populist attitudes across our three elections – 2008, 2012, and 2016 – then, in somewhat more detail, some social correlates of these attitudes. We should be clear that none of these are panel studies; ultimately, only longitudinal analysis can provide a satisfying demonstration of the stability of populist attitudes according to the ideational approach. While there is some preliminary panel survey data from Europe for one or two countries, no such data exist yet for the United States.

For all samples, our measure of populist attitudes is an unweighted average of answers to an item inventory created by Akkerman et al. (2014) and earlier by Hawkins et al. (2012). The inventory asks respondents "how much you agree with each of the following phrases" and then presents a series of populist-sounding sentences that get at the core components of populism, including a Manichaean outlook, people-centrism, and anti-elitism. The full six-item Akkerman inventory has been shown to scale somewhat poorly at the extremes, where it struggles to distinguish extremely high versus high populist attitudes, and it is not as reliable for cross-country comparison as newer item inventories (S. M. Van Hauwaert, Schimpf, and Azevedo 2019). However, it does well at distinguishing individuals in the middle of the scale, and its cross-country reliability is still acceptable (Castanho Silva et al. 2019). Because different surveys have used different response scales (4-, 5-, and 7-point), responses for all of our datasets have been rescaled to 0 (not populist) to 1 (populist).

Because the 2008 preelection and 2012 postelection US surveys lack the full six items, we present the full scale in just the 2016 survey. For all other US and foreign surveys, and for comparability also in the 2016 US sample, we draw on three items: "The politicians in Congress need to follow the will of the people"; "The people, not the politicians, should make our most important policy decisions"; and "What people call compromise in politics is really just selling out on one's principles." The other three items of the full scale are "The political differences between the people and the elite are larger than the differences among the people"; "I'd rather be represented by an ordinary citizen than an experienced politician"; and "Politicians talk too much and take too little action."[8]

---

[8] For the three items, Cronbach's alpha is somewhat lower than in international studies using the full index: 0.69 for the 2016 study, 0.57 for 2012, and 0.67 for 2008. (And we do recognize that Cronbach alpha's use is not ideal with three items.) For the full six items, used only in one model for 2016, alpha is 0.80, identical to levels found in other countries.

The 2016 US study was an online survey using a nationally diverse sample of 840 respondents created by Qualtrics, with quota sampling based on gender, age, education, and partisanship to match averages from the US Census.[9] The survey was part of an experiment in which subjects answered a series of open-ended questions about problems in the United States, but the populist attitude items were asked pre-treatment. The 2008 and 2012 studies were also online surveys, both modules of the Cooperative Congressional Elections Study with 1,000 respondents each. While the 2008 study was a nationally representative, preelection sample, the 2012 study was a nationally diverse, postelection sample.

Figure 5 compares basic descriptive statistics for the three US samples with the results from eleven other countries: nine European (Switzerland, the United Kingdom, Germany, Sweden, Poland, Spain, France, Italy, and Greece) and two Latin American (Bolivia and Chile). While one of these is an urban sample (Bolivia, from the four largest cities), all others are nationally representative.[10]

Because we have speculated that populist attitudes are driven by a broader democratic culture in combination with other personality traits, variation within countries should be much greater than variation across countries, and overall levels will be high. The results in Figure 5 confirm this. Levels are all similarly high, with nearly all responses in the upper end of the scale. The largest difference in means across countries is 0.07, between Greece (0.64) and Switzerland (0.73); although statistically significant (as we would expect with such large samples), this is substantively very small. More to the point, the differences in means across countries is much smaller than the typical standard deviation within countries – around 0.18. In other words, most of the variation is within countries. Admittedly, Figure 5 shows that average levels of populist attitudes are not identical across the fourteen samples. There is even a possible pattern: the United States in 2016 and the Catholic countries of Latin America and Southern and Central Europe are all higher than the Germanic countries of Northern Europe and the United States in earlier years, suggesting some kind of cultural difference. But given the dramatic differences across these countries in

---

[9] Regression analyses do control for these variables to overcome sampling bias.

[10] All of the European data come from an online survey conducted by the LIVEWHAT Project on a sample of 18,368 respondents, +/- 2,000 per country, in summer 2015. The survey, which was carried out by YouGov, uses a quota sample based on gender, region, age, and education (S. Van Hauwaert and van Kessel 2018). The Chilean data come from the 2013 United Nations Development Programme preelection survey, a face-to-face survey of 1,800 respondents surveyed with probability proportional to population, stratified by region and zone (urban/rural); the resulting margin of error is 2.5 percent with 95 percent confidence, and the design effect is 1.15. The Bolivian survey was conducted by IPSOS in June 2016. It was a face-to-face survey of 1,060 respondents in households in the cities of La Paz, El Alto, Cochabamba, and Santa Cruz (Andreadis et al. 2019).

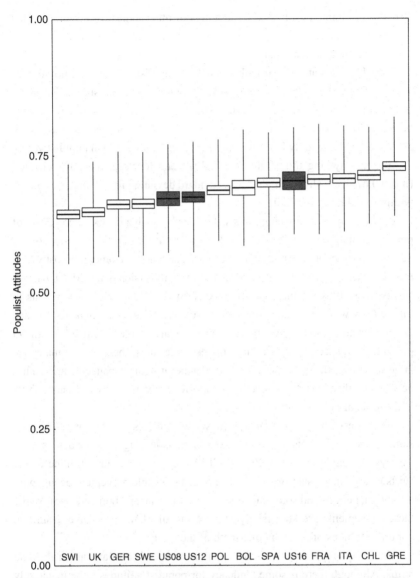

Figure 5 Average populist attitudes from a comparative perspective (scale 0–1). The box-and-whisker plot shows the mean level of populism, along 95 percent confidence intervals around the mean (box) and with the sample size independent one-standard deviation of the responses around that mean (whiskers) to highlight the degree of variance within the countries. US samples are highlighted in gray.

Note: In Figures 1, 3, and 4, boxes denote the standard deviation and whiskers the confidence intervals. In this plot we reversed that since the large survey sample sizes (versus the number of content analyzed speeches) yielded small confidence intervals and large standard deviations.

terms of economic development and a host of other indicators – including the presence of populists in government – the similarity in the distributions of populist attitudes is remarkable.

In the United States in particular, levels of populist attitudes are not dramatically different from what we find elsewhere. Levels of populist attitudes are all in the upper half of the scale. Results show a statistically significant increase between 2012 and 2016, from a mean of 0.67 to 0.70, but the increase is not substantively large, only 0.03. We could not ascribe the surge in populist voting in 2016 to anything this slight, especially when levels in the 2008 election (mean 0.67) were already high.[11] The standard deviation for all three samples is within rounding error: 0.20.

Another way of approaching this stability is by analyzing social correlates of populist attitudes. We calculate this by performing an OLS regression of six indicators on populist attitudes: age, gender, education, income, religiosity, and race. For these we include both a three- and six-item version of the 2016 Qualtrics survey, as well as the three-item indexes from 2012 and 2008. The results in Figure 6 show the estimated effect of a two-standard-deviation-change in each continuous independent variable leaving dummies untransformed,[12] with 95 percent confidence intervals around the estimate; thus, these are estimates for large shifts in each social correlate. Note that because the dependent variable has been standardized to a 0–1 scale, the x-axis effectively indicates percentage shifts in the scale of populist attitudes.

The clearest finding is the relative consistency of these coefficients. Although some of the coefficients move in and out of statistical significance across these surveys, especially between 2012 (CCES) and 2016 (Qualtrics), none of the shifts is large in substantive terms. The most noticeable movement occurs with education, gender, and some categories of race (Asian and nonresponse). While these movements are statistically significant, all of them involve a shift in populist attitudes of less than one-tenth of the scale.

What is equally impressive is how small these social correlates are in absolute terms. Although there is some tendency for populist attitudes to be negatively associated with education, income, and certain racial categories (African-Americans, Hispanics, and Asians have lower populist attitudes than whites) and positively associated with age, religiosity, and being male, together these

---

[11] We are wary of claiming that there is even a difference between the population mean of the 2016 and earlier US samples given that the 2016 survey was done quite far from the elections with a different sampling strategy making it less comparable. Confidence intervals also overlap.

[12] Gelman and Hill (2007, page 57) suggests this scaling is the most comparable between continuous and dummy variables. Such a uniform scaling of continuous variables also helps to roughly compare the corrected magnitude of the effect across variables.

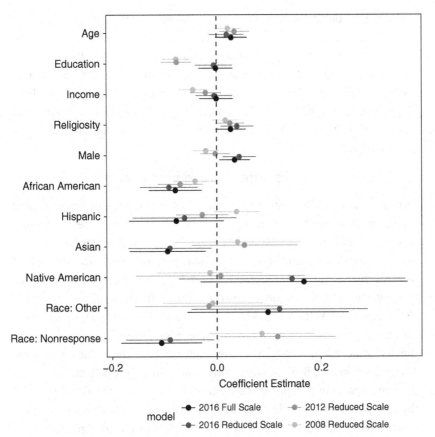

Figure 6 Predictors of populist attitudes (scale 0–1). Coefficients show the percent shift with either a categorical (for dummies) or two-standard-deviation change (for continuous) of the predictor along with their 95 percent confidence intervals. Sample size and adjusted R^2 for 2016 full scale = 565/0.06, 2016 reduced scale = 565/0.05, 2012 reduced scale = 849/0.05, and for 2008 reduced scale = 956/0.06.

explain very little of the variation in populist attitudes. The adjusted R^2 for each of these models is only between 0.05 and 0.07. Not only is the profile of people with populist attitudes fairly stable (again, insofar as we can tell without true panel data), but it is hard to predict who these people are with basic social and demographic data. We suspect much of the variation in populist attitudes reflects more fundamental differences. Very little work has been done in this realm to date, but several scholars are turning to psychological dispositions as causally prior phenomena for explaining the variation in populist attitudes. Elchardus and Spruyt (2016) highlighted the importance of anomie in explaining populist attitudes. Silva et al., testing a large number of plausible psychological mechanisms, found that individuals with a high level of populist attitudes tend to think the world is unfair and filled with essentially evil people and that they are very certain (highly dogmatic) of such beliefs (Silva et al. 2018). Populist attitudes' relationship to conspiratorial thinking has also been suggested, though the causal direction here is not clear-cut (Silva, Vegetti, and Littvay 2017). Unfortunately, we are unable to test any of these correlates with these datasets.

Populist Attitudes and Vote Choice

While generally in line with other comparativists' findings, the strong, stable presence of populist attitudes in the United States (not to mention across countries and regions) highlights a puzzle: if populist attitudes are so wide-spread, how come populist parties are not more common? The strength of populist parties varies considerably across these twelve countries. Some had very strong populist parties in government at the time of these surveys (Greece under SYRIZA and ANEL, and Bolivia under MAS), while others had comparatively mild populists in government (Poland, Switzerland), and finally some did not have any (the United States, the United Kingdom, Germany, Sweden, Spain, France, Italy, and Chile). Despite lacking a populist government in the United States, the populist supply was already offered by vice-presidential candidate Sarah Palin in 2008, the Tea Party and Occupy Wall Street in 2012, and by Trump and Sanders in the 2016 primary race. Other countries without populist governments (or only mild ones) also had populist opposition parties present (Front National in France, Progressive Party in Chile) or emerging (AfD in Germany, Podemos in Spain, 5-Star Movement in Italy), and, although not a party, the Brexit movement in the United Kingdom is also potentially comparable to the Tea Party or Occupy Wall Street in its populist character and organization. Still, in few of these cases did strong populist attitudes consistently translate into populist electoral success.

The answer is that populist attitudes predict vote choice and other forms of political behavior, but only among the segment of voters with active attitudes – and the size of this segment depends heavily on context. The principal way that comparativists have tested this argument is by running vote choice or vote preference models, using populist attitudes as a predictor after controlling for other standard explanations such as issue positions and political ideology. Individuals with stronger populist attitudes are more likely to vote for populist parties, but only if those parties are also ideologically proximate. And the more the context lends itself to the activation of these attitudes, the more of the vote that these attitudes will explain.

Because vote-choice analyses are a relatively new test for the ideational approach, it may help if we review what they have found. To begin with, all studies show that populist attitudes (often measured using some of the same items presented here) are significant predictors of vote preference for populist parties. Importantly, these attitudes predict support for both left- and right-wing variants of populism, showing that there is a similar ideational phenomenon that undergirds all types of populism and that these ideas are shared by ordinary voters (Akkerman, Zaslove, and Spruyt 2017; Andreadis et al. 2019; S. Van Hauwaert and van Kessel 2018).

Beyond this there are some inconsistent or weaker findings. First, very few individual-level studies take context into account. Just one, a two-country study of populist voting in Greece and Chile (Hawkins, Rovira Kaltwasser, and Andreadis 2018), shows that overall levels of "populist voting" (the percent of the overall vote explained by populist attitudes) are much higher in Greece than in Chile, even though overall levels of attitudes are the same in both countries. While this fits the different contexts of these countries (widespread corruption and systematic policy failure in Greece versus relatively mild representation deficits in Chile), two cases are certainly not enough to draw a generalizable inference on the country level. The proposition that corruption is the relevant mechanism is also not tested at the individual level through, for example, measures of perceived corruption.

Second, there are stronger but contradictory findings concerning the proposition that populist attitudes will interact with other issue positions, i.e., that populist attitudes only explain support for parties among voters with issue positions that already match those of the parties. One study that pools data across eight countries (using some of the same LIVEWHAT data presented in Figure 5) fails to find a strong interactive effect (S. Van Hauwaert and van Kessel 2018), but a study of the Netherlands, the aforementioned study of Chile and Greece, and a four-country non-pooled study of Chile, Bolivia, Greece, and Spain all find clear interactive effects (Akkerman, Zaslove, and Spruyt 2017; Andreadis et al. 2019; Hawkins, Rovira Kaltwasser, and Andreadis 2018).

Within the United States, there are just two studies that explore the effect of populist attitudes, both for the 2016 presidential election. The first, a study by Oliver and Rahn of the primary election, finds that populist attitudes (using Oliver and Rahn's own inventory) help predict support for Trump and less so for Sanders; however, no interaction is tested. The second, a study by Rahn of the general election using the ANES populism module (a series of items designed for the 2015–2020 round of the Cooperative Study of Electoral Systems), again finds an association of populist attitudes with voting for Trump, although the effect dissipates once a full battery of issue positions are controlled for; interaction effects are tested with null results.

To replicate and extend these comparative results in the United States, we perform a vote choice analysis for the 2016 primary campaign and test support for Occupy Wall Street and the Tea Party in the 2012 general election using the data presented earlier (Qualtrics and CCES samples). For 2008, despite Sarah Palin's vice-presidential nomination, there are unfortunately no instances of populist outcomes we measured with our survey.[13]

For 2012, we model two different measures: support for Tea Party and support for Occupy Wall Street. Although these use four-point scales for outcome (strongly favorable, somewhat favorable, somewhat unfavorable, extremely unfavorable), for ease of presentation and comparability with the 2016 models we use OLS. Note that this is the first time anyone has studied the impact of populist attitudes on the Tea Party or Occupy movements – or for that matter, the impact of populist attitudes on any US movement prior to 2016 (cf. Arceneaux and Nicholson 2012; Formisano 2012; Karpowitz et al. 2011; Rasmussen and Schoen 2010; Skocpol and Williamson 2013). Although there is some dispute, many scholars see the Tea Party and Occupy movements as instances of populism, thus providing us with a unique opportunity to gauge support for organized instances of populism in an earlier election (Lowndes 2017; Mudde and Rovira Kaltwasser 2017).

In both models we add controls for key explanations of the Tea Party and the Trump phenomenon that Americanist scholars often conflate with populism: authoritarian attitudes (2012 and 2016, using the child-rearing inventory), attitudes toward immigration (2012 and 2016, but using different measures), and racial resentment (available in 2016 only). We show that even beyond these explanations, a thin-ideological formulation of populist attitudes, void of ideological content, has strong explanatory power and should be considered to understand key political outcomes in US politics and beyond.

Our main predictor in all models is the populist attitude index. For the 2012 survey this is again the three-item version, but for all 2016 analyses we use the full six items.

Results for these models are in Figure 7. Interestingly, populist attitudes do not predict support for Occupy Wall Street. Although a populist movement in its rhetoric and championed later by Bernie Sanders, the most clearly populist

---

[13] If we could go back in time and add just one question to any of these surveys, it would be a feeling thermometer of Sarah Palin in 2008.

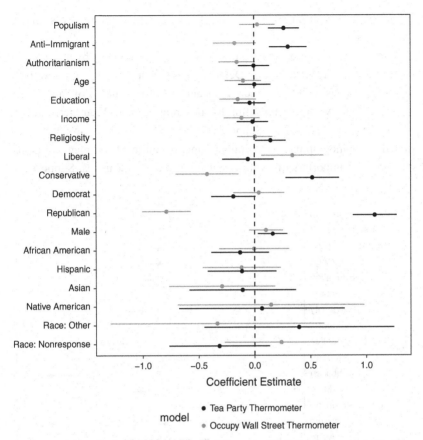

Figure 7 Predictors of Tea Party and Occupy Wall Street support (1–4) including populist attitudes. Coefficients show the shift as predicted by either a categorical (for dummies) or two-standard-deviation change (for continuous) of the predictor along with their 95 percent confidence intervals. Sample size and adjusted R^2 for Tea Party = 544/0.64 and for Occupy Wall Street = 524/0.41.

politician with ample visibility in US politics, Occupy Wall Street had primarily ideological appeal. It was perceived more favorably by liberals and less favorably by conservatives (vis-à-vis moderates). Additionally, the educated, authoritarians, and people with anti-immigrant sentiments had a much more negative perception of the movement. It comes as little surprise that Occupy Wall Street was less supported by Republicans compared to independents and Democrats. While other tendencies are also visible from the graph, none of them reach statistical significance.

The picture is different for the Tea Party. This not only had a stronger populist appeal, seen in the statistically significant effects of the populist attitude index, but a broader one. It was not seen as negatively by liberals and only to a much lesser extent by Democrats as Occupy was by conservatives and Republicans. Otherwise the results appear mirror images of each other. The Tea Party was most appealing to conservatives and Republicans (even controlling for each other). Support for the Tea Party was also better predicted by demographics, with higher support coming from men, religious people, and supporters of stronger anti-immigration measures. Support for

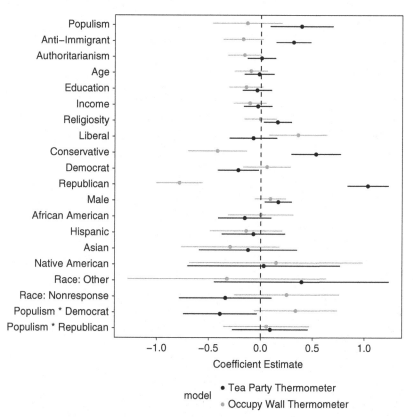

Figure 8 Predictors of Tea Party and Occupy Wall Street support (1–4) including populist attitudes and its interactions with partisanship. Coefficients show the shift as predicted by either a categorical (for dummies) or two-standard-deviation change (for continuous) of the predictor along with their 95 percent confidence intervals. Sample size and adjusted R^2 for Tea Party = 544/ 0.64 and for Occupy Wall Street = 524/0.41.

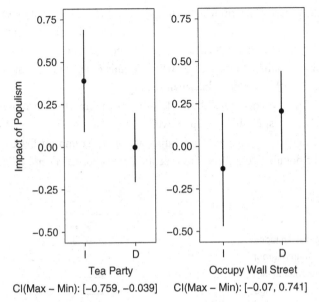

Figure 9 Marginal effects plot of populism's impact on Tea Party and Occupy Wall Street thermometer (0–100) for Democrats versus independents. Coefficients show the percent shift for two-standard-deviation change in populist attitudes for Democrats and independents, along with their 95 percent confidence intervals.

the Tea Party was about 20 percent more predictable based on the R^2, which could simply be a result of its relative prominence and recognition as a movement by the public.

While these results are somewhat satisfying, in that they find a link between populist attitudes and support for one of these two movements, the ideational theory suggests that these attitudes must be filled up with ideological content. For this reason, we would expect different kinds of populists to appeal to Democrats and Republicans, in line with the ideologically different nature of these two movements. To test this, we reran the previous models interacting populism with party ID (using independents as the reference group). The results show that the interaction between being a Democrat and populist has a significant impact on both Tea Party and Occupy Wall Street (only $p < 0.1$) sympathies in the expected direction. In essence, this means that populist Democrats disliked the Tea Party even more than their non-populist counterparts, further lending credence to the theory that ideological content matters beyond populism. Interestingly, for Republicans the interaction effects are not mirrored, suggesting that the Tea Party's populist appeal cut across party lines.

For 2016, our first set of dependent variables is feeling thermometers for the three strongest populist candidates: Trump, Cruz, and Sanders; we run separate models for each thermometer using OLS. As before, our most important predictor is the populist attitude index, which, in this case, is built using all six of the items from the original Akkerman scale.

Results for the unconditional models are in Figure 10. The most striking finding is that despite their comparatively high populist rhetoric, neither Cruz nor Sanders seems to appeal to populist attitudes. Trump on the other hand gathers the populist vote. With the exception of authoritarianism, other factors

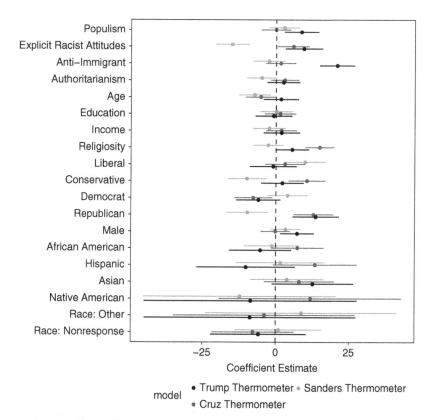

Figure 10 Predictors of candidate thermometers (0–100) including populist attitudes. Coefficients show the percent shift predicted by either a categorical (for dummies) or two-standard-deviation change (for continuous) of the predictor along with their 95 percent confidence intervals. Sample size and adjusted R^2 for Trump = 504/0.31, Cruz = 506/ 0.25, and Sanders = 506/0.29.

identified by Americanists also matter. While anti-immigrant sentiments have the strongest effect on Trump support, explicit racial attitudes matter roughly as much as populist attitudes, highlighting how important this omitted variable is. Additionally, Trump appeals most to men, unsurprisingly Republicans, and more surprisingly Asians ($p < 0.1$) and the religious. Conservatives do not seem to approve of Trump. Cruz has an even stronger religious and a distinctly conservative appeal. Republican partisanship predicts his support as strongly as Trump's. Cruz also receives support from people with explicit racial prejudice, though the same is not true for people who support anti-immigration measures. Cruz's support is also higher among Hispanics ($p < 0.1$). These two results could possibly be explained by his last name and Cuban refugee father. Unsurprisingly, Sanders is most popular among young people, liberals, people who do not exhibit racial prejudice and those who are low on authoritarianism, but conservatives or Republicans do not like him.

Curious about the lack of populist appeal for Sanders, we once again ran an interactive model (Figure 11) to see if Sanders' appeal is stronger among Democrats who are populist. Here now we find a populist appeal among Democrats. As compared to independents, Sanders' populist appeal is sizably and significantly larger and also, as shown in the marginal effects plot of Figure 12, significantly different from 0. Interestingly, Trump's populist appeal does *not* interact with partisanship or any other control, and Cruz's support is still unassociated with his populism.

The ideational theory suggests that populism, in itself, is quite a nondescript empty signifier and needs to be filled up with issues and ideology that populism helps frame. In the models presented in Figures 8–12, this ideological content was proxied by partisanship mainly to maintain comparability with the following section where we compare primary vote (where voters vote within their own party). But a more direct test of the theory would be to let populism interact with ideology rather than partisanship . This is exactly what we do in Figures 13 and 14.[14]

Based on these results it becomes clear that Trump has almost equally strong appeal for both liberal ($p < 0.1$) and conservative ($p < 0.1$) populists but much lower appeal among the reference group of moderate populists. Sanders' appeal among liberal populists is statistically significant at traditional $p < 0.05$ levels.

Finally, beyond the thermometers, we have at our disposal a more direct measure of candidate support: vote intention. But we need to assess these responses carefully. It is important to remember that, in most states, it is only

---

[14] In 2012, this model yielded no significant interactions.

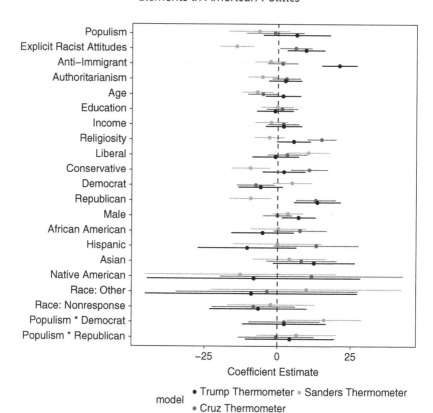

Figure 11 Predictors of candidate thermometers (0–100) including populist attitudes and interactions with partisanship. Coefficients show the percent shift as predicted by either a categorical (for dummies) or two-standard-deviation change (for continuous) of the predictor along with their 95 percent confidence intervals. Sample size and adjusted R^2 for Trump = 504/0.31, Cruz = 506/0.25, and Sanders = 506/0.29.

Democrats who vote in the Democratic primary and Republicans who vote in the Republican. So all of these assessments need to be considered in the framework that a vote for or against Trump is a vote by a Republican in a primary. It is also important to note that the analysis has less power due to the dichotomous nature of the outcome and the limited sample of primary voters further spliced by nonparticipation in the primary and the partisan nature of primary voting. For these reasons, it is no surprise that the results of this analysis do not mirror the thermometer results exactly. With this in mind, let's take a look. Needless to say, partisanship is not controlled for as the samples are split by partisanship anyway. We present four sets of results: a primary

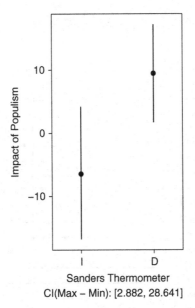

Figure 12 Marginal effects plot of populism's impact on Sanders' thermometer (0–100) for Democrats versus independents. Coefficients show the percent shift for two-standard-deviation change in populist attitudes along with their 95 percent confidence intervals.

vote for Trump, for Cruz, for any of one of these two populist Republican candidates, and for Sanders. Figure 15 highlights the results from the logistic regression.

It seems clear that in all cases (with the exception of a primary vote for Cruz) populist attitudes did, in fact, predict the respondent's candidate choice. Racial attitudes in this analysis didn't have a significant impact, but anti-immigration sentiments separated both Trump (with a positive sign) and Cruz (with a negative sign) supporters significantly. When pooling the two, anti-immigration attitudes had a positive effect, highlighting the dominance of the stronger effect for Trump voters. Authoritarianism, once again, did not matter in the way expected by Americanists; rather it was a Sanders vote that authoritarianism predicted negatively. Indirectly, this suggests that Clinton supporters were more authoritarian (which makes sense as she was the establishment candidate supported by those who followed the party without objection). Older people were less likely to vote for Sanders, highlighting his strong support among young people. People with higher education were more likely to vote for Sanders. With the exception of Cruz, religious people were less likely to vote

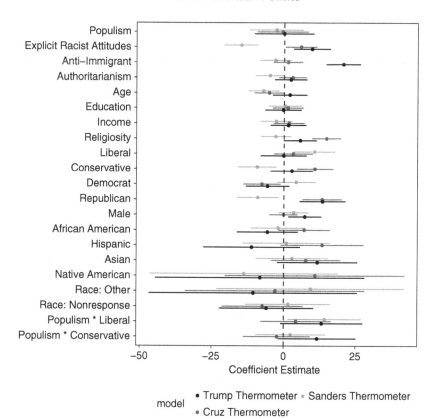

Figure 13 Predictors of candidate thermometers (0–100) including populist attitudes and its interactions with ideology. Coefficients show the percent shift as predicted by either a categorical (for dummies) or two-standard-deviation change (for continuous) of the predictor along with their 95 percent confidence intervals. Sample size and adjusted R^2 for Trump = 504/0.32, Cruz = 506/0.25, and Sanders = 506/0.29.

for a populist candidate (Cruz bucked this trend with statistical significance). Looking from the perspective of the primary, interestingly, gender did not have an effect on the primary vote with the exception of Sanders, who gathered men's support (probably because his main opponent was a woman).

Overall, we think the comparativists have got the picture of populism right. Not only are populist attitudes in the United States as strong and stable as in other countries, but populist attitudes correlate in predicted ways with most of the candidates from the 2016 primary and with two putative populist movements in 2012. Furthermore, if we have got this picture right, the analysis

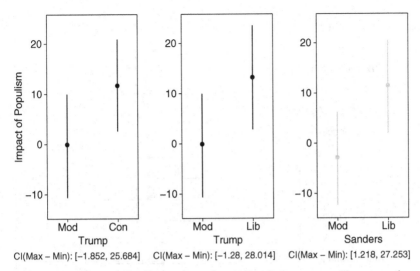

Figure 14 Marginal effects plot of populism's impact on Trump and Sanders' thermometers (0–100) for the significant interactions: Liberals versus Moderates versus Conservatives. Coefficients show the percent shift for two-standard-deviation change in populist attitudes along with their 95 percent confidence intervals.

provides some important details about the populist appeal of these candidates and movements. Trump's populist appeal in 2016, in contrast with that of Sanders, was spread across the ideological and partisan spectra. This broad appeal would have mattered for Trump's vote once he moved from the primaries into the general election and may clarify the widespread understanding that Trump appealed across party lines to Democratic voters in Rustbelt states. Perhaps this cross-party appeal was heavily populist, driven by these voters' appreciation not just for his policy positions but for his particular populist take. Unfortunately, our survey data are not fine grained enough for this to be more than speculation. One thing is clear. The explanatory factors often conflated with populism – authoritarianism, racial resentment, and anti-immigration attitudes – although important, do not negate the impact of populism. In fact, populism's impact on Trump's support is comparable in magnitude to that of explicit racial attitudes. At the same time, though there are no surprises here, these explanations do not work for Sanders, the most populist candidate of the 2016 primaries. This is why it is important not to conflate populism with its ideological content.

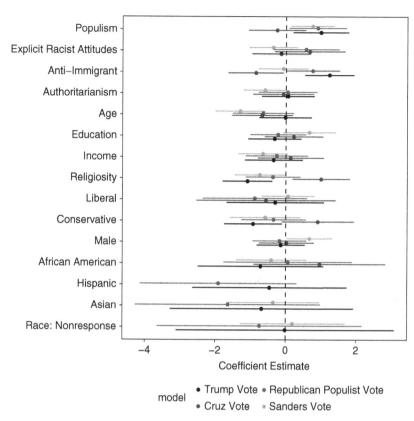

Figure 15 Predictors of primary vote including populist attitudes (logistic regression). Coefficients show raw logistic regression coefficients for the dichotomous outcome as predicted by either a categorical (for dummies) or two-standard-deviation change (for continuous) of the predictor along with their 95 percent confidence intervals. Note that coefficients with extremely high uncertainty (usually in cases when inference for a dichotomous predictor was based only on a handful of people) hindered visualization of the more interpretable results and are omitted from this figure. Sample size for Trump = 191, Cruz = 191, Republican populist vote = 191, and Sanders = 222.

A lingering question is to what degree these results speak to the impact of broader context, one that remains relatively constant though a single country lens. We said at the beginning of this section that Trump and other populists in the 2016 campaign emerged under conditions of high economic growth and low corruption that are, at best, only somewhat propitious to populist voting. It is also important to remember that this populist moment is a noteworthy but comparatively mild case. The United States in 2016 was not Greece or

Venezuela with their highly dysfunctional, corrupt political systems, but perhaps Spain with its relatively recent economic crisis and corruption scandals. This is difficult to test systematically with just our US data, but we will just point out that having populist attitudes two standard deviations higher than the mean, or practically speaking being at the first versus second tercile, make a Republican around 2.5 times more likely to vote for Trump or populist Republican candidate and a Democrat twice as likely to vote for Sanders.

Experimental Evidence

The ideational argument makes another unique set of predictions concerning the impact of populist rhetoric on voters' attitudes and behavior. Because ideational scholars emphasize the importance of populist rhetoric for activating citizens' populist attitudes, they try to identify the components of this rhetoric and connect them to theories of political psychology and communication. Roughly four components have been suggested (Busby, Gubler, and Hawkins 2019; Hawkins and Rovira Kaltwasser 2019). First, populist rhetoric works by interpreting policy failures as a democratic normative threat. It argues that a given policy failure has a much greater impact than just harming our material interests but that it embodies a danger to democratic values of equality before the law. While we presume that the objective circumstances of a policy failure need to be serious in order to be interpreted as this kind of normative failure, the point is that the rhetoric helps voters make this connection, reminding them of policy failures and pointing out their consequences. Second, populist rhetoric encourages people to attribute blame for these failures. Specifically, it engages in dispositional attribution rather than situational attribution, blaming knowing agents (the elite) rather than impersonal circumstances or events outside anyone's control. Third, populist rhetoric primes and reinforces certain in-group identities, those connected to one of our main political communities – the mass of citizens who embody our democratic virtues – as opposed to more local or apolitical groups such as one's neighborhood or occupational group. Finally, populist rhetoric incorporates language priming certain emotions, especially anger. These emotions not only accompany active populist attitudes but may independently facilitate or catalyze a populist framing of issues.

Comparativists have conducted a few experimental studies of these mechanisms, although that number is rapidly growing with the new attention on populism. One of their findings is simply that populist rhetoric matters for attitudes and behavior. When subjects read about political issues, they have a very different response (including increased vote intention for populist parties) when these texts are framed using populist language (Bos, Van Der Brug, and De Vreese 2013; Matthes and Schmuck 2017; Rooduijn, van der Brug, and de Lange 2016). Other studies try to move beyond this and test individual components of the rhetoric. For example, these find that mentions of corruption around even ordinary policy issues can encourage the expression of populism and make people more willing to work with individuals using populist rhetoric (Busby et al. 2019), that rhetoric has a powerful effect on populist attitudes when it involves some kind of attribution (Hameleers, Bos, and de Vreese 2016), and that priming anger arouses populist attitudes in subjects, while priming fear has no effect (Rico, Guinjoan, and Anduiza 2017).

Few experiments on populist rhetoric have been performed in the United States, let alone the 2016 campaign (e.g., Busby et al. 2019). However, with another colleague, we conducted an experiment in the course of our 2016 Qualtrics survey. The analyses presented here, so far, excluded all study participants who received a populist prime in the experiment, but now we bring these people back and analyze the impact of blame attribution on candidate support. This experiment is described in more detail elsewhere (Busby, Gubler, and Hawkins 2019), but we think it is helpful to summarize some of its findings because of their link to the presidential campaign. In the study, we presented two groups with a list of current "problems in our country" and asked them to identify which one they considered most serious. Subjects were then asked one of two sets of open-ended questions, each of which was designed to encourage a different type of blame attribution. In one, modeling situational attribution, subjects were asked "which events or circumstances" were to blame for the problem and what should be done about them. In the other, subjects were asked "which groups or individuals" were to blame and what should be done about them. A third group of subjects was not presented with any of these questions – problem selection or open-ended responses – and served as a pure control. These treatments were administered before the questions on the feeling thermometers.

Our expectation was that those asked about groups or individuals (dispositional attribution) would be more likely to prefer a populist candidate to a non-populist one. To test this, we rerun (and present in Figure 16) the impact of the dispositional blame attribution treatment on the feeling thermometer models for Trump and Sanders. We consider both the absolute thermometer scores for Trump and Sanders and the difference between the feeling thermometer of these two candidates and Clinton. Results point to an impact that is most pronounced (and significant) using the difference scores for Trump. Even a very simple one-time message appears to have an effect on the likability of a populist versus a non-populist presidential candidate.

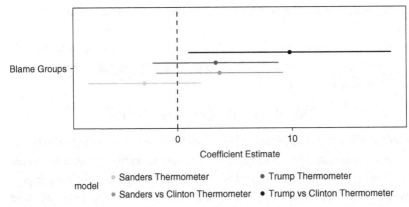

Figure 16 The impact of a blame attribution treatment for the country's problems on candidate thermometers (scale 0 to 100 and −100 to 100 in the case of thermometer difference). Coefficients show the absolute shift. Treatment and control group sample sizes for Trump = 270/564, Trump versus Clinton = 270/563, Sanders = 273/566, Sanders versus Clinton = 273/565.

All in all, it appears that the mass-level findings in the comparative populism literature hold for the American context. Now that the American voters decided to elect a populist president, in the next section we take a look at what happens to countries where the head of the government is populist. We use the comparative models to forecast the expected impact of American populism.

4 The Consequences of Populism and How to Mitigate Them *with Saskia P. Ruth, German Institute for Global Area Studies*

If populism exists as a set of ideas among political elites and ordinary citizens, and if it helps explain voting and other behavior, what are its consequences for politics and policy, especially when populists take office? Even before Trump's election, pundits and scholars talked about his negative impact on American democracy, including the polarizing effects of the campaign and the license it provided for uncivil discourse. These concerns have intensified in the face of attacks by the president of the media and independent government agencies, as well as an increasingly poisonous and sometimes violent civic discourse between Trump's opponents and supporters.

In this final section we address these concerns in two ways. First, we measure populism's impact on liberal democracy – and talk about which of the possible scenarios the United States today is likely to fit into. Second, we identify what the comparative research tells us about mitigating populism's negative consequences. Because the latter is a relatively new area of comparative research, it is also more speculative, and we suggest avenues for further research for comparativists and Americanists.

Populism and Liberal Democracy

Scholars and pundits often assume that populism is bad for all kinds of political and economic outcomes. There is still a widespread sentiment that it harms the economy (Acemoglu, Egorov, and Sonin 2013), although most newer perspectives on populism call this presumed link into question (Roberts 1995; Weyland 1999); this link may reflect the unique features of left-populism in regions such as Latin America. Highlighting the potential endogeneity problem with populism's correlates, a few people argue that populism leads to corruption, an ironic outcome given that populism is likely a response to the perceived abuse of state resources for private gain (Heinrich 2017).

While evidence for these effects is still scanty (for an analysis of populism and economic outcomes, see Houle and Kenny 2018), one of the clearest findings from comparative research concerns the impact of populism on liberal democratic institutions, or the institutions of democracy that protect minority rights and prevent tyranny while still ensuring popular participation. Populists in opposition can provide a wake-up call to traditional politicians that reshapes the public agenda and increases political participation; indeed, some populist politicians expressly pursue the political inclusion of previously excluded groups, such as through institutions of direct democracy (Canovan 1999; Huber and Ruth 2017; Mudde and Rovira Kaltwasser 2012). But once in power, populists erode checks and balances, curtail civil liberties, and undermine the fairness of electoral competition (Huber and Schimpf 2016; Houle and Kenny 2018). This democratic rollback is often checked by domestic and international institutions as well as the populists' own lingering concern for popular sovereignty – populism genuinely values elections for the seal of popular approval they provide and they often celebrate popular democratic participation – so the rollback usually falls short of full autocracy. Competitive elections and most civil liberties persist, and a nominal separation of powers remains. The result is a kind of competitive authoritarianism where the opposition cannot fairly compete and alternative voices are increasingly silenced (Bogaards 2009; Krekó and Enyedi 2018).

Populism also results in polarization (Handlin 2018; McCoy, Rahman, and Somer 2018). The concern here is not so much with ideological polarization, or the increasing distance among voters in terms of their issue positions or traditional ideology, a topic of lively debate among US political scientists (Abramowitz and Saunders 2008; Fiorina, Abrams, and Pope 2008). Rather, the problem is affective polarization, or mistrust and intolerance for one's political opponents as members of an out-group (Iyengar, Sood, and Lelkes 2012). Affective polarization has many sources, but populism is a pernicious one. It demonizes opposition voters as accomplices of the elite, eschews compromise, and questions liberal democratic institutions that protect rights of people with minority viewpoints. Populists do not see opponents as worthy, legitimate competitors, but as enemies. The opponents of populists respond in kind. Because opponents feel threatened and attacked, they denigrate populist politicians and their supporters, such as Clinton calling Trump's supporters a basket of deplorables, and shut them out of the political spaces they still control. Obviously, this plays into the populists' fears of elite conspiracy, justifying further attacks and harsher rhetoric. Citizens and politicians caught in the middle are forced to choose sides to avoid being lumped in with an opposing party, potentially explaining how Trump brought so many Republicans over to his side so quickly. This polarizing dynamic makes peaceful democratic competition difficult and can tear communities apart.

Let's take a look at a few non-US cases. For several years after his election in 1999, Chávez had widespread support of Venezuelans because of his perceived effectiveness at addressing economic and political inequality. His government instituted reforms designed not merely to redistribute the country's oil wealth but to make the political institutions more participatory and responsive, such as community councils for distributing community infrastructure projects or constitutional provisions for recall and referenda. However, these improvements were ultimately overwhelmed by the government's efforts to enshrine Chavismo's legacy and protect the people's will from its supposedly sinister opposition. Although Venezuela's slide to autocracy was only completed under Chávez's successor after 2013 (by 2016 it was listed by Freedom House as "not free"), Chávez imposed constraints on civil liberties and electoral fairness, and he steadily concentrated power in the executive branch. For example, private media were silenced through censorship laws, withdrawal of government advertising, withdrawal of government licensing, and outright purchase through third parties; the country's nonpartisan election commission was filled with loyal appointees who set election dates favoring the government and overlooked the government's violations of campaign laws; and the judiciary was repeatedly stacked with partisan appointees, while unfavorable rulings to the government resulted in death threats and imprisonment for wayward judges.

While heavily nationalist tendencies were present since World War I when Hungary lost 2/3 of its territory, historically Hungary also had a strong consensual political culture. Both of these cultures manifested visibly in the country's early years of post-Communism. Despite the newly acquired freedom of speech, giving irredentist ultra-nationalist groups the opportunity to make enough noise to gain broad visibility, the governing elites definitely swung toward a consensus culture of political leadership. The first government of Hungary in 1990 was comprised of a reasonably broad coalition. The Hungarian Socialist Party in 1994 was unwilling to govern alone despite securing over 50 percent of the parliament. Even in coalition with the Liberal Free Democratic Union, which together held a 2/3 majority in parliament needed for constitutional change, the two parties decided not to produce a new basic law unless an opposition party signed off. None did. However, after the economic crisis of 2009 hit Hungary and the dishonest practices of the governing socialists were documented in a famous leaked speech, Orbán and his Fidesz party won decisive control of the parliament. Despite widespread protests, Fidesz upended Hungary's culture of consensual political culture and initiated an institutional overhaul that included the single-handed writing of a new constitution, a new media law severely limiting press freedoms, and an overhaul of the judicial branch with new limits on its independence from the executive branch. Fidesz also put in place a new election system that helped maximize the party's share of parliament. The government was reelected in 2014 and 2018 with 2/3 seat shares despite receiving fewer votes and smaller vote shares than in 2010. After each election they demonstrated their power by eroding institutions historically in place to check government power. For example, after the 2018 election, Fidesz passed laws limiting the political maneuverability of civil society organizations and their ability to raise funds.

Turkey completely decimated its party system following an economic downturn; in the 2002 general election, the Turkish people ousted 100 percent of their parliament. This led to the rise of the Islamist and highly personalistic Justice and Development party (AKP) and its leader, Recep Tayyip Erdoğan. In his first term, Erdoğan was not especially populist, striking instead a relatively pluralist tone. Furthermore, he delivered high economic growth and expanded the welfare system as well as civil rights. However, at the start of his second term Erdoğan become much more populist in his discourse. He also began to forcefully eliminate potential competition by jailing anti-Islamist generals, including his former chief of staff, on the grounds of alleged coup plans. By 2010, through a referendum, he changed the constitution to curb the independence of the judiciary, which had repeatedly attempted to limit his powers. Erdoğan's new enemy became a mostly invisible informal network led by Fethullah

Gülen, an Islamic cleric living in self-imposed exile in the United States. Initially Erdoğan considered Gülen a close ally, especially in dismantling the anti-Islamist wing of the military, but after a 2013 corruption scandal that embarrassed the party, Erdoğan blamed the scandal on an international conspiracy led by Gülen and began claiming that Gülenist forces intertwined government institutions, AKP, and the Turkish people. Any evidence of Erdoğan's wrongdoing, whether the demolition of a park or leaked tapes incriminating evidence of his own or his government's wrongdoing, was blamed on this invisible network of evil elites. In 2016, Erdoğan faced an actual but unsuccessful coup attempt that gave him the excuse to purge his remaining political enemies. Authorities suspended or fired over 100,000 government employees (including replacing most elected mayors with appointees), jailed more than 60,000 people, shut down over 1,000 civil society organizations, and severely curtailed press freedom. A subsequent referendum – criticized for widespread violation of campaign laws – further centralized power in the presidency.

Comparativists and political theorists provide two explanations for these patterns. One draws from standard rational-choice arguments about vote-maximizing politicians. Populist politicians always define themselves as political outsiders with few connections to the political establishment, and they run on a platform of overturning the establishment. By working with established politicians and bureaucrats, these outsiders risk alienating their voters. Furthermore, for populists who are actual outsiders, working with traditional politicians, independent agencies, and bureaucrats is relatively difficult because they cannot build off any existing relationships. Such outsiders have relatively more to gain and less to lose by undermining checks on executive power and using incendiary language to demonize and repress their opponents (Levitsky and Loxton 2013).

The other explanation builds on the ideational approach. It suggests that many politicians and voters actually believe the populist message of a corrupt establishment and a righteous popular will. For such politicians, it becomes imperative to curtail their opponents' access to democratic institutions, because these opponents are a united enemy bent on harming the polity for its selfish purposes, not an actual opposition. Thus, civil liberties such as freedom of expression or the right to assemble must be withdrawn or extended only conditionally. Furthermore, because there is just one right way of doing things, the people's way, and this correct path is knowable to all those who are in contact with the popular will, there is less need for fully open electoral competition (Abts and Rummens 2007; Urbinati 1998). Finally, if the popular will is successfully embodied in a charismatic leader, government institutions should be designed to see the leader's will into law, not to check and balance it with multiple, independent points of view.

All of this paints a pretty dark picture for a country like the United States that has just come under the sway of a populist leader. But the warning signs pre-date Trump. Antiestablishment sentiment was prevalent, to some extent, since Gingrich's 1994 Contract with America and clearly moved to the forefront of Republican politics since the emergence of the Tea Party (Medzihorsky, Littvay, and Jenne 2014). During this time Bush governed as if nothing has happened. Palin struck a chord with these sentiments in 2008, but Romney in 2012 ran on a platform that ignored the anti-government grievances the Fox News era had created. Polarization increased all this time, and there has been a weakening of institutions and checks and balances for political gain (political use of impeachment against Bill Clinton, curbing of civil liberties through the Patriot Act under Bush, the regular use and subsequent elimination of the filibuster, and the unprecedented obstruction of Merrick Garland's nomination), all of which further diminished the respect for democratic norms, as well as approval of Congress and even the Supreme Court (Browning 2018). It is little surprise that the next stop on this road was the strengthening of populist candidates both on the left and the right. It would be difficult to argue that things did not get worse under Trump. Indeed, early results of the Bright Line Watch survey show a decline in both the public and academic's perception of how well American democracy was performing after Trump's election (Bright Line Watch 2018).

However, properly situating these processes in the United States also requires careful comparative analysis. Not only can we be a bit more precise with our estimates of populism's effect, but we need to take into account a few con-textualizing factors, including the level and type of populism and how long the populist has been in office.

To provide this perspective, we analyze the correlations between a variety of indicators of democracy and our earlier data on populist discourse of chief executives. We show only bivariate comparisons – with one exception, which we show in Figure 17, the basic trends do not change when we run these as multivariate analyses. The x-axis of each figure measures the level of populist discourse for each leader-term, with the scale running from 0 to 2. Trump's first year is not included as a data point – he hadn't been in office long enough to register a shift in democracy indicators – but his average level of populism is highlighted with a gray vertical line. In the y-axis we show two different measures depending on the graph: on the left, the absolute level of the indicator at the end of the term; and on the right, the level of change in the indicator, calculated from the beginning of the leader's first term to the

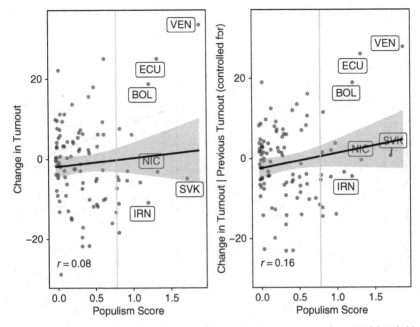

Figure 17 Bivariate impact of populism on voter turnout for presidential/ parliamentary elections (including 95 percent confidence interval). Figure on the right includes initial level turnout as a control to account for ceiling effect. Turnout is measured using the International IDEA database (original scale 0 to 100 percent). Populist attitudes measured with qualitative text analysis on a scale of 0 to 2. The vertical line shows where Trump is on populism. Especially interesting countries are highlighted with their three-letter ISO codes. Correlation is not significant for the figure on the left and significant at $p = 0.11$ for the figure on the right.

end of the last.[15] We include both versions of these democracy indicators – level and change – to determine whether populism leads inexorably to full autocracy or if it simply results in a decrease from whatever point the country was at.

Results can be found in Figures 17–21. Overall, the patterns affirm the potentially positive impact of populism on participation and the clearly negative impact on other aspects of liberal democracy. To measure the impact on

---

[15] For voter turnout, we calculate the change from the election *before* the leader's first victory to the last election in which he or she ran as an incumbent. For most leaders, the last election is the one that ended their first and only term.

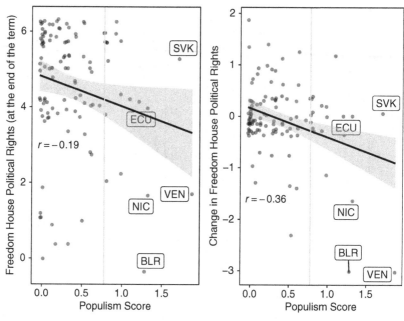

Figure 18 Bivariate impact of populism on Freedom House's Political
Rights index, a broad measure of electoral fairness and competition
(original scale of 1–7 is reversed so that 7 indicates the maximum
democracy – the figure includes 95 percent confidence interval). Populist
attitudes measured with qualitative text analysis on a scale of 0 to 2. The
vertical line shows where Trump is on populism. Especially interesting
countries are highlighted with their three-letter ISO codes. Correlation is
significant for both figures.

participation, we examine the association of populism with (change in)
voter turnout (Figure 17). We find that the simple correlation between
turnout and populism is essentially nil. However, when we control for
ceiling effects (model not shown here), a modest positive pattern emerges.
Countries with strong populist leaders experience larger increases, or at
least lower decreases; in fact, the largest increases in the dataset are under
strong populist leaders. Almost all of these increases are limited to populists in Latin America. This may confirm arguments by comparativists that
left populists increase participation more than right populists because of
their appeal to low-socioeconomic status groups (Mudde and Rovira
Kaltwasser 2013a).

The results for indicators of democratic contestation are more sobering. The
left-hand sides of Figures 18–21 do not show much consistent correlation
between populism and absolute levels of democracy – the relatively flat

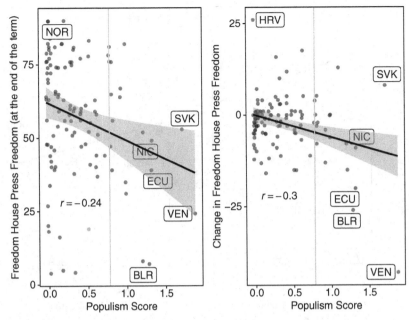

Figure 19 Bivariate impact of populism on Freedom House's Press Freedom index (original scale of 1–100 is reversed so that −100 indicates the maximum press freedom – the figure includes 95 percent confidence interval). Populist attitudes measured with qualitative text analysis on a scale of 0 to 2. The vertical line shows where Trump is on populism. Especially interesting countries are highlighted with their three-letter ISO codes. Correlation is significant for both figures.

trendlines in these figures show that populist governments end up in a variety of places. Populism does not always end in full-blown autocracy. But the right-hand figures clearly show a negative relationship between populism and changes in democracy; the higher the level of populism, the more negative the impact. These declines are statistically significant and considerable in size. If we consider the best-fit line, the decrease is on the order of 1 point for political rights (again, on a 7-point scale), 10 points for press freedom (100-point scale), 3 points for polity2 (20-point scale), and 1 point for executive constraints (7-point scale). These patterns are not limited to Latin American governments but include governments such as that of Lukashenko in Belarus. Furthermore, we should bear in mind that these are only average estimates of populism's impact. If we consider the actual decreases under the most notorious and highly populist governments, such as those of Chávez or Lukashenko, the declines are often two or three times larger.

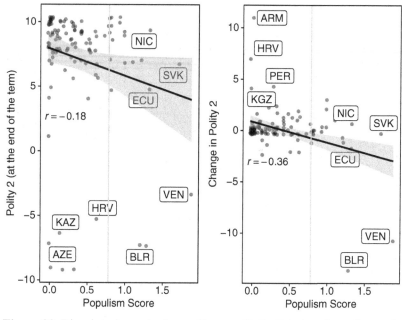

Figure 20 Bivariate impact of populism on Polity2 index from Systemic Peace, a measure of democratic performance (original scale from −10 to +10 where +10 indicates maximum democracy) – the figure includes 95 percent confidence interval. Populist attitudes measured with qualitative text analysis on a scale of 0 to 2. The vertical line shows where Trump is on populism. Especially interesting countries are highlighted with their three-letter ISO codes. Correlation is significant for both figures.

What does all of this mean for the United States after 2016? Regarding participation the outlook may seem positive. Trump and other candidates helped legitimate the views of many voters who felt forgotten and brought their concerns onto the public agenda – a development that we would argue was generally positive. Post-election analyses suggest that turnout increased slightly among certain groups as well, especially white voters, although the aggregate increase was not much different from previous elections (File 2017).

However, there are a few caveats that suggest this populist moment may have less of a lasting, positive impact on participation. First, as already noted, the increases in voter turnout in Figure 17 are most noticeable among left populists such as Chávez, Correa, and Morales. Trump's appeal to forgotten constituencies was initially limited to white blue-collar workers and tended to exclude poor racial minorities such as African-Americans that left populists would have

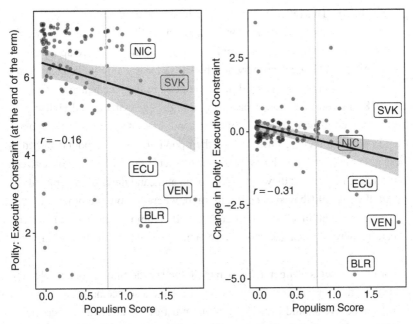

Figure 21 Bivariate impact of populism on Polity2 index of executive
constraints, also from Systemic Peace, an indicator of checks
and balances on the executive branch (original scale of 1–7, where
7 indicates the maximum democracy) – the figure includes 95 percent
confidence interval. Populist attitudes measured with qualitative
text analysis on a scale of 0 to 2. Gray line shows where Trump
is on populism. Especially interesting countries are highlighted
with their three-letter ISO codes. Correlation is significant for
both figures.

reached out to. Second, the techniques that populists use to increase turnout are
not always fair or legal. In the case of Chavismo, for example, the government
"bought turnout" by granting citizenship to immigrants with minimal require-
ments, by providing targeted public goods, and by monitoring (coercing) the
participation of suspected supporters on voting day (Rosas, Johnston, and
Hawkins 2014; Kornblith 2005). To the degree that we are seeing anything
like this under Trump, it seems to be in the negative. One thinks here of the
Republican Party's ongoing efforts to make voting more difficult with stringent
registration and voter ID laws, which disproportionately hit poor families and
especially racial minorities that tend to vote Democrat. Third, some of the
increase in turnout in other countries comes from opposition supporters showing up to defend government institutions from a perceived hostile takeover by

populist forces. This reflects a high-stakes, polarized environment – not the kind of regular, sustainable participation envisioned by liberal theorists. While the results in the Senate (where only very few Republican seats were up for grabs) and the swing in House seats may not show it so clearly at first glance, in terms of raw voters Democrats showed up at the polls in unprecedented numbers in the 2018 mid-term election, recapturing a highly gerrymandered House with unprecedented turnout. And finally, after some of these populist governments were in power for a long time and saw their popularity slip, turnout declined as these governments found themselves with smaller cohorts of supportive citizens to mobilize, more so as they repressed voters and candidates of the opposition. Again, the case of Chavismo comes to mind, where turnout plummeted to well under 50 percent in elections after 2017. If Trump loses his own voters' affection, there is little reason to believe their levels of participation will remain high.

For other aspects of liberal democracy in the United States, such as election quality or the separation of powers, the outlook also seems mixed. On the positive side, we should bear in mind that most of the countries experiencing high levels of populism today were not unblemished democracies to begin with, and populists encountered weaker resistance from government institutions and civil society (although Venezuela was a more institutionalized democracy than we like to remember now). Institutions in the United States, such as term limits, the presence of strong independent agencies, and a professionalized bureaucracy (nowadays vilified as the "deep state"), impose barriers to populist ambitions. Likewise, the democratic rollback under populists takes time. Although not shown in Figures 17–21, the greatest declines in democracy (and increases in participation) typically occur in the second or third terms in office and are spread over several years; these are not coups, but gradual, piecemeal changes. Finally, as the reference line in the figures reminds us, the United States after 2016 still had low to moderate levels of populism; none of the countries in this range have experienced large declines in democracy.

Yet there are ominous signs. Media freedom and checks and balances have already born the brunt of Trump's attacks, with critical media dubbed as "fake news" and explicit actions against journalists, along with efforts to remove heads of government agencies that threaten the president and his agenda. Also, most voters who identify as Republican (about 25 percent of the electorate) remain staunch supporters of Trump's conduct in office. And while our analysis of Trump's campaign discourse reveals low average levels of populism, this is because he has a limited belief in the will of the people, not because his speeches frequently strike a pluralist tone; his antiestablishment discourse is stronger and more consistent. Thus, while we are among the voices that see America's democratic institutions as a check on the potential negative effects of populism (Mickey 2017; Weyland and Madrid 2017), we think the data give justifiable cause for concern.

Needless to say, these analyses are also quite limited. The models are hardly specified fully. The tests are correlational and potentially suffer from endogeneity that limits our ability to make mechanistic causal claims.[16] And while our hypotheses are the appropriate ones today in light of the 2016 presidential election results, they only consider the populism of governments. What about a populist opposition? One could easily imagine a different outcome for the 2016 presidential election with Clinton winning, if dominant forces in the Republican Party continued to pursue a populist approach. But who is to say these are not already the right questions today? The "opposition" was certainly populist during the 2016 general election once Trump and Cruz emerged as the frontrunners. Embodied by the Tea Party (and, to a lesser extent Occupy Wall Street), a populist opposition was already present under Obama. These topics call for additional empirical exploration. Mudde and Rovira Kaltwasser (2012) hypothesized that populism in opposition had the potential to improve substantive representation, suggesting that some populism in the party system was desirable, yet Huber and Schimpf (2016) tested this proposition in Europe without finding any evidence. We still have little comparative evidence to go on.

Mitigating Populism

What could mitigate these negative consequences? The ultimate mitigation is to eliminate the underlying problems that give rise to populism. For most developing countries, this means creating honest, efficient bureaucracy and eliminating practices of vote-buying and patronage – a tall order to be sure, but one that development scholars and international organizations have pursued in recent decades (Abed and Gupta 2002; World Bank 1997). In wealthy democracies such as the United States, however, eliminating populism's underlying causes is not so straightforward. A naïve approach to populism in the wealthy democracies would be to coopt the populist platform, adopting populist policy objectives without the populist rhetoric. Clearly, this is problematic. Depending on the ideological flavor, populists in these countries call for closing borders to immigration, ending open markets, and withdrawing from international organizations. It is not clear that most citizens in these countries actually support these positions, which populists may be adopting strategically as a way of

---

[16] See Houle and Kenny (2018) for a methodologically creative attempt to overcome the endogeneity problem in a study of populism in Latin America and the Caribbean.

signaling their antiestablishment goals. Adopting these platforms wholesale would also mean giving up on core principles of American liberalism and spell disaster for the global economy.

Comparativists are aware of these concerns and offer three other routes to mitigation. These are (1) *containing* populism's impact through resistance by domestic and international actors; (2) *waiting out* the inevitable decline in support for populist forces, since anti-elitism leads to incompetence in governance that eventually undermines popular support; and (3) *engaging* in measured policy responses that acknowledge the core of the populist complaint, but without giving in to its contradictory excesses.

To be clear, the study of populist mitigation lies at the frontier of populism studies. While there are a number of theories speculating about the forces that check or channel populist impulses, rigorous empirical tests of these ideas are slim. Most of them focus on the state level of analysis or the international system, with little on the psychology of populism or on local-level techniques for mediating conflict in polarized societies. Also, most of this research is still somewhat perversely focused on the *causes* of populism, rather than on effective *responses*. In particular, there is very little study of alternative discourses to populism, especially pluralism, or why some populist governments eventually lose power. All of this suggests directions for future research by both comparativists and Americanists.

Containing populism. The first type of mitigation – and the one that has received the most study – is containment by state- and system-level actors. International actors, including other states, nongovernment organizations, and international organizations, may be able to check the democratic misbehavior of populists in power by supplementing or backing the efforts of domestic actors such as independent institutions, opposition politicians, and civil society (Bozóki and Hegedűs 2018; Rovira Kaltwasser and Taggart 2016).

Containment comes in varying degrees of respect for liberal democratic norms, ranging from military coups and legal prohibition of populist challengers (some of which obviously end democracy in their own way) to lawsuits, sanctions, and nonviolent protests. Country studies show that stronger forms of containment do not work in practice; populist forces tend to grow anyway, and outright prohibition fuels the populist argument by demonstrating that the traditional political elite really is conspiring against the populists. These stronger forms of containment suggest that traditional politicians lack confidence in the power of their own ideas. Moreover, fighting fire with fire contradicts liberal democratic principles of freedom of speech and association, not to mention the need for a level playing field in elections. Ultimately, strong forms of containment reflect a profound misunderstanding of what is driving support for populism, blaming the irrationality of citizens (and hence the need to forcibly constrain them), rather than the failures of the liberal democratic system to represent all of its citizens blind to socioeconomic status, gender, race, religion, or political conviction, and treat them as equals before the law. At the end of the day, populists are not (at least initially) extremists that advocate the use of violence and reject the need for peaceful elections. The best solution to populism is not to forcibly prevent it from coming to power.

However, especially if populists come to power, liberals should not stand by and watch as populists dismantle liberal institutions and create their own lopsided set of rules. If populists break or attempt to do away with the rules, international and domestic actors can use softer forms of containment short of outright prohibition. For example, international actors can speak out against and punish these actions as violations of core democracy principles, activating provisions for the protection of human rights. Efforts here can go beyond shaming and include more concrete actions, such as finance and shelter for persecuted domestic actors, economic sanctions, and even expulsion from regional associations. One thinks here of efforts by the European Union to sanction efforts by the Polish government to curtail judicial independence, or the international response to the Orbán government's efforts to shut down Central European University. Opponents of the Chávez government initially found refuge in rulings from the Inter-American Court of Human Rights. Given the size and power of the United States, these international actors can only have a limited effect as compared to their impact on smaller countries, but they hold resources that can make a difference at the margins.

A better bulwark against populist excesses in the United States are domestic actors, including independent government agencies, opposition parties, and civil society. Populism's negative impact on democracy usually takes time, and control over government institutions is often limited initially to the executive branch. Independent agencies such as the judiciary should stand their ground, knowing that capitulating to demands for constitutional reforms is unlikely to placate populist forces and will instead be used to gain piecemeal control over the state. Opposition parties must move quickly to reform internally and position themselves to respond positively to the populist platform. Ordinary citizens should organize, protest, and lobby at the absolute first warning signs to ensure that their institutions are not curtailed. All of these actors can respond to populist aggressions with a pluralist discourse that avoids the trap of a polarizing rhetoric that demonizes populists.

The bad news is that when populists in power are highly radical and there is broad electoral support, the impact of international and domestic actors on democracy is limited. In countries such as Venezuela and Ecuador, where highly populist presidents were in power a long time, efforts to halt the negative impact of populism on democracy were largely ineffective (de la Torre and Ortiz 2015; Hawkins 2016b). In Venezuela in particular, where oil revenues provided unusual latitude to the Chávez government and its successors, the government ignored rulings by international commissions and courts and eventually withdrew from them. In Ecuador, the negative impact of the Correa government was only blunted when Correa left office and his chosen successor, Lenin Moreno, turned out to hold more liberal views.

The good news for the United States is that these efforts at mitigation are more effective in countries where the populists in power are more moderate or have less than majority support (Fallend and Heinisch 2016; Stanley 2016). This may be because the populists themselves are internally constrained by liberal democratic beliefs and strong democratic institutions, but it may also be because there is less backing from voters for highly radical departures from democratic norms; the opposition is larger and better able to coordinate its actions, and even populist supporters may be relatively moderate. It may also result from the inexperience and bad decisions of populists who are relative political newcomers.

Most of these conditions currently prevail in the United States. Levels of populist voting are not as high as in countries such as Greece and Venezuela, and the conditions for the emergence of radical populists – systematic misconduct, illegal political behavior and state failure – are not present. The Trump administration has struggled to find its voice and to express it through effective rule. And the opposition is still largely united in a single party. While we discussed these factors as potential causes for the rise of populism, once the head of government becomes a populist, we can also rely on these factors to mitigate populism's negative consequences. However, we reemphasize that this should not come as complete reassurance. Domestic and international actors also must remain active, vigilant, and respond to transgressions, knowing they will occur and grow worse if left unchecked.

Engaging with populism. A more viable and, we would argue, essential technique for mitigating populism is engaging with the underlying grievances that fuel the populist message and polarize the public. By this, we do not mean adopting an equally populist counter-rhetoric or merely coopting populists' policy positions. Instead, we mean trying to understand the underlying policy concerns and the apparent (or real) democratic deficits that transform concerns into failures of representation. Much of this is a matter of listening respectfully to populist voters and publicly acknowledging the legitimate aspects of their concerns. Taking this approach not only addresses populism's underlying causes but also potentially reduces affective polarization.

Ideational approaches to populism argue that populist rhetoric is usually directed at real grievances that violate democratic norms of citizenship and equal rights before the law. The attitudes of populist voters are activated when they believe that policy failures are the result not just of impersonal forces or well-meaning, incompetent politicians but of systematic elite collusion against their interests. If the opponents of populists can identify the source of these grievances and publicly acknowledge their legitimacy, without necessarily giving up their political positions, they may defuse the populist argument while identifying compromise policy solutions.

For example, populist frustrations with economic globalization are often a response to real failures of politicians to provide meaningful trade adjustment or build social services capable of reaching citizens who are disadvantaged by an open economy and technological innovation. These gaps in government assistance could be addressed. Yet traditional politicians have chosen not to do so, preferring to reinforce the problem without implementing adequate policies of trade adjustment or building a better social safety net (Berman 2017; Colgan and Keohane 2017). Thus, there is a measure of elite responsibility to which populists can legitimately point. For non-populists who want to preserve an open economy for their community and enjoy the benefits of globalization, the application of the principle of engagement requires publicly acknowledging the legitimacy of the populist complaint and pursuing better trade adjustment policies while still promoting trade openness. Simply *recognizing the truth* in the populist complaint could send a powerful message and create space for non-populists to defend liberal democratic principles.

Likewise, while immigration to the US and other wealthy democracies can address humanitarian concerns and bring economic and cultural benefits through the infusion of labor and ideas, not every citizen is in a position to reap these benefits. For people who have to live and work with neighbors from a very difficult culture, or who face difficult competition for employment and government services, immigration seems to generate mostly costs. When politicians fail to adopt policies that address these imbalances, ensuring that all citizens share equally in immigration's benefits, they open themselves up to the charge that they are systematically advantaging some citizens at the expense of others. This is a potentially serious violation of liberal democratic norms (Colgan and Keohane 2017; Galston 2018). Again, openly acknowledging the legitimacy of these concerns could go a long way toward defusing populist arguments. If non-populist, pro-immigration politicians publicly affirm the rule of law and the concerns of potentially disadvantaged citizens in policy discussions, they may reduce tensions and create space for promoting the kind of immigration necessary for the economy as well as humanitarian outreach.

Unfortunately, non-populist actors, not to mention the media, often fall captive to the polarizing dynamic of populist discourse and are unwilling or unable to show this empathy, tending instead to dismiss populist politicians as demagogues and their followers as irrational or immoral. This has certainly been true in the United States since 2016, where some Democrats have blamed their loss on turncoat partisans and moderate Republicans while expressing condescension toward Trump followers. This only makes things worse. Clearly, affective polarization among US voters predates the 2016 election (Iyengar and Westwood 2015), but recent evidence (Iyengar and Krupenkin 2018) and the pattern in other countries suggest it will become much worse under populism.[17]

Research on the effectiveness of rhetorical engagement is still somewhat scant. For example, a venerable strain of research on the psychology of conflict argues that efforts to humanize opponents are important tools for reducing conflict (Batson and Ahmad 2009). One form of humanization that seems promising is reciprocal empathy, or validation. When members of an out-group are seen as expressing empathy for the in-group – that is, recognizing the in-group's viewpoint and experience as legitimate – members of the in-group reduce their feelings of hostility (Gubler, Halperin, and Hirschberger 2015). However, very little of this has been applied to the study of affective polarization under populism. While a few country studies describe this process of polarization (Handlin 2017; McCoy and Diez 2011), almost none include research at the individual level to determine what aspects of populist rhetoric have this effect and how they connect to related attitudes of voters, such as tolerance and trust.

One reason for this lack of evidence is that too much populism research still focuses on the causes of populism, rather than its solutions: what rhetorical tactics reduce negative views toward political opponents and foster dialogue, especially under populist governments. Yet the ideational approach points out discourses such as pluralism that offer alternative modes of political discussion. Presumably, the response to populism is not to avoid discussing the important

---

[17] Although affective polarization in the United States seems to precede and accompany the emergence of populism in 2016, this is not the situation in other countries where populists have recently come to power. In countries such as Venezuela, Hungary, Greece, and Italy, populists emerged in situations of ideological convergence among the traditional parties, and large numbers of voters were united in their disapproval of incumbent governments. Affective polarization followed the emergence of populist forces, which demonized their opponents and provoked a defensive counterreaction (Roberts 2019).

issues it raises, but to discuss them differently. A few experimental studies show that such alternative rhetorics work (Busby, Gubler, and Hawkins 2019; Hameleers, Bos, and de Vreese 2016), in the sense that they allow discussion without raising populist hackles, but whether these are practical in the real world is still something we know little about. This requires a conceptual and theoretical framework in which populism can be situated alongside other -isms.

Waiting out populism. A frequent hope of opposition parties once populists come to power is that if they wait long enough, the populists will simply go away, and everything will return to normal. We think this outlook is naïve and shows an unwillingness to engage with the problems that bring the populists to power in the first place. It is, unfortunately, common in developing countries where parties are dominated by patronage machines and political leaders who lack the incentives or tools to engage in policy innovation and organizational renewal. Fortunately, in wealthier democracies with programmatic party competition, politicians face a different set of incentives and constraints. Certainly, there seems to be little sitting around right now in the United States, and both moderate Republicans and Democrats are taking care to reach out to their constituents and show genuine interest in their concerns over issues such as economic opportunity and the conflict between traditional values and progressive secularism. However, there is something to be said for waiting and seeing how the populists fare in government, since strategic blunders and weak performance may provide critical opportunities for opponents to move.

Hence, an important area of research is the study of how populists stay in power – and why some of them lose it. In fact, both sides of this coin contain puzzles. Some populists keep control of government institutions for years, even with policy performance that would turn other parties out of power. Many of the familiar examples of populism we have mentioned are leaders who stayed in power for two or more terms, sometimes in the midst of economic downturns. Chávez in Venezuela, for example, suffered from a sluggish economy during his first 2–3 years in office and witnessed another gradual downturn toward the end of his second term, shortly before going on to win reelection. We cannot blame these leaders' longevity merely on the adoption of autocratic institutions, because most of these leaders stayed in power through elections (if slightly unfair ones) with significant support from the electorate. Viktor Orbán of Hungary was frequently criticized for adopting election rules to favor his own party (Fidesz), but the reality is that both elections under the new rules would have been won by Fidesz under any electoral system.

Thus, populist incumbency is not well explained by standard Americanist models of voting behavior, especially economic voting. At a minimum, populists seem to enjoy a cushion that dampens the effect of economic voting, quite possibly due to populists finding various elites (be it international organizations or the banking sector) to blame the economic downturn on, legitimately shifting the blame in the eyes of their supporters.

However, explanations for populist longevity do not come so easily from comparativists either. The ideational approach to populism suggests that other dimensions of political beliefs are at work – that voters may support a populist leader even during economic hard times and poor government performance if he still seems to honestly care about the people and can persuade them that the enemies of the people are hard at work against them. But aside from vote choice analyses, like those we have performed here for the United States in 2016, there is little exploration of this dimension. In fact, few vote choice analyses or analyses of presidential/executive approval have been done for *incumbent* populists, especially studies incorporating populist attitudes (but see the analysis of Bolivia in Andreadis et al. 2019). The problem is not just empirical but theoretical. There are still no formal spatial analyses that incorporate a populist dimension, nor is it clear how a strict Downsian rational choice perspective can be readily accommodated to a perspective emphasizing citizens' normative beliefs or notions of dignity.

We also lack studies of when populists lose power. Again, it is easy for scholars to obsess over the rise of populists and to rehash the process that brings them into government (witness this Element), but we are not fully leveraging our data unless we consider the cases in which populists fail and leave office. We might imagine this happening through violence, such as a popular uprising or a military coup. This was often the case for mid-twentieth-century populists in Latin America, such as Juan Domingo Perón in Argentina, who was removed from power in 1955 after a series of violent anti-government demonstrations and a military coup. Erdoğan faced a coup attempt in 2016 as well, as did Chávez in 2002. But in recent years this transfer of power from populist to non-populist is just as likely to take place through formal impeachment processes and/or regular elections as it has several times now in Brazil (e.g., Collor de Melo in 1994), Argentina (Carlos Menem in 1998), Ecuador (Correa in 2017), and Italy (Berlusconi in 2006 and 2011). However it happens, the point is that populists are not eternal and we should be studying why they lose power.[18]

---

[18] Case studies of populism in other countries offer some clues. Quite a few populists are brought down by evidence of corruption. In Peru, for example, right-populist Alberto Fujimori fled the country and resigned after a series of televised videos showed his chief assistant bribing dozens of legislators. Likewise, some leaders may not have much talent or resources for governing. This was the fate of Abdalá Bucaram, a populist in Ecuador who alienated his supporters through poor choices for cabinet ministers and his support for economic policies that harmed his constituents.

5 Conclusion

Americanists should no longer ignore the study of populism. Missing this academic conversation was always unproductive. As our data and other studies have shown, populist forces certainly exist in the United States today and have done so throughout the past century or two even. Ignoring the existence and impact of populist ideas in the 2016 campaign means that we miss a major part of the causal story. Levels of populism among the candidates reflected a gap in representation, one that we can fully grasp only if we understand the nature of populist claims concerning the normative failures of political representatives. Likewise, populist attitudes in the electorate were not active for every voter, but they were an important determinant of voting in addition to partisanship and ideology. Given these results and the availability of methodological and theoretical tools, there seems little reason to continue excluding populism and other political discourses from the toolkit of empirically minded Americanists.

But missing this academic conversation is also perilous. It is true that the effects of populism on American democracy are yet to be fully experienced – Trump has only been in power a couple of years, and he is only moderately populist (but Sanders is a true populist and while his ideological positions are less exclusionary and hence arguably more in line with liberal democracy, had he come to power and not Trump or if a Democrat like Sanders comes to power after Trump, many of the ills of populism, such as affective polarization, could be amplified well beyond what we see today).

Studies of populists in power in other countries show consistently the negative impact of populism – and not just its particular ideological manifestations – on core institutions of liberal democracy. While the jury may still be out for the effects of populism on macroeconomic performance or corruption, and while populists may have beneficial consequences for participation and democratic representation, populists in power are responsible for some of the most serious cases of democratic backsliding over the past two decades. Again, scholars should be cautious in estimating the effects of populist government on consolidated democracies, and we are sympathetic to voices that suggest a more optimistic view in the United States due to its strong independent and democratic institutions. We are also painfully aware of the real inequities in contemporary American politics that justify populist complaints. But Americanists should not draw too many lessons from past populist third-party movements in their own country, most of which never came to power or exercised their full impact on American institutions.

If Americanists accept the challenge of incorporating populism into their toolkit, this Element will have served half its purpose. But the other half is to persuade our colleagues that comparativists have much to offer and that collaboration might be the best route. This requires implementing, not reinventing conceptual, methodological and theoretical wheels. While the techniques we have applied here are not the only tried and tested tools for studying populism, they represent a set with a good track record of performance. There are usually good reasons for adopting these tools rather than others – certain types of textual analysis fit populist discourse better, for example, and certain batteries of items for measuring populist attitudes have already been shown to generate more accurate ranges of measures across multiple countries; large datasets are already available for large-N analysis and cross-country comparisons. Creating and promoting entirely new tools or promoting conceptual redesigns that ignore previous work may provide short-term payoffs, but it is a poor use of scarce scholarly resources and will likely yield little to no long-term impact. Let's spend the resources gathering data useful both for American politics research and also the kind of comparison that is the hallmark of comparative political research.

More to the point, common tools allow us to share data and make comparisons that, we hope we have shown here, provide useful perspective. Clearly, there is room for improvement in the comparativists' techniques or the theorists' definitions for studying populism, but both of these have advanced enough to provide pretty good measures that work across time and space, including the space called "the United States." Some readers may feel frustrated by an approach showing that a particular candidate or president is not as populist as they thought, but adopting this approach allowed us to reveal oscillations of Trump's rhetoric that gave insight into his character and behavior. Adopting these kinds of universal standards also allowed us to ask why the United States doesn't have as much populism as some Latin American countries today, or to make more accurate assessments of the impact of populism on American political institutions. We worry about US-centric approaches that offer sensationalist accounts of populism. Adopting comparativist approaches to populism can be a recipe for better, more careful science. And as we have personally experienced in our cross-regional studies and large-scale analyses, the work with large numbers of scholars from other countries is incredibly gratifying.

Does this mean populism is the only thing worth studying in US politics today? Obviously not. Donald Trump's rise was certainly a multi-causal occurrence. The American public's receptivity to Trump's moderately populist messages is an important factor, as was the earlier emergence of the Tea Party pushing similar populist messages, the amplification of these messages by media that could hardly get enough of Trump's sensationalism, and the

Democratic Party's response to Trump, which initially involved dismissing and vilifying his supporters (we can think of Hillary Clinton's joke about the "basket of deplorables" during the campaign).

Still, there were other factors at play. Far too many people saw the Obama presidency as something that should be avenged for reasons that had more to do with ideology and identity politics than populism. What better way to do this than to elect the person who most effectively questioned the legitimacy of the Obama presidency? Likewise, for a decade and half we have known that a large segment of the American public seeks the simplicity they see in corporate organization structure – the sentiment that government should run more like a business headed by benevolent executives with centralized power to get things done along with clear accountability (Hibbing and Theiss-Morse 2002). Trump certainly was not the first presidential candidate who fulfilled this promise, but he was the most successful. Finally, ordinary partisanship and, again, ideology (technically orthogonal to populism) played important roles. Once Trump became the nominee of the Republicans, many people simply voted for the more conservative of the two viable general election candidates. Bringing populism into the toolkit of Americanists does not mean we should throw away the other tools; it means we should use them together.

But one of the best reasons for Americanists to study populism together with their comparativist colleagues is that comparativists also have a stake in what happens in the United States and would like to have this conversation with their Americanist colleagues. This is true not only for the comparativists who live in the United States, but for political scientists living in other countries for whom the United States is an extremely important case of comparative politics, and who inevitably feel the effect of US politics on what happens to them at home through the policies and example set by America, whether it be trade, democracy and human rights promotion, immigration, or international security. In many countries these scholars are experiencing their own forms of polarization rooted in left- and right-populism, and they are hoping for ideas and solutions to come from their colleagues. It is disheartening for them to see how the United States has further polarized, even tribalized, on just about every issue, and they would like to help. When Americanists acknowledge these scholars as friends and allies, they will find powerful research toolboxes and fruitful collaborations that will advance the study of the American case with more rigor, rooted in a stronger foundation of research.

References

Abed, George T., and Sanjeev Gupta, eds. 2002. *Governance, Corruption and Economic Performance*. Washington, D.C.: International Monetary Fund.

Abramowitz, Alan I., and Kyle L. Saunders. 2008. "Is Polarization a Myth?" *The Journal of Politics* 70 (2): 542–55.

Abts, Koen, Thierry Kochuyt, and Stijn van Kessel. 2019. "Populism in Belgium: The Mobilization of the Body Anti-Politic." In *The Ideational Approach to Populism: Concept, Theory, and Analysis*, edited by Kirk A. Hawkins, Ryan Carlin, Levente Littvay, and Cristóbal Rovira Kaltwasser. London: Routledge.

Abts, Koen, and Stefan Rummens. 2007. "Populism Versus Democracy." *Political Studies* 55 (2): 405–24.

Acemoglu, Daron, Georgy Egorov, and Konstantin Sonin. 2013. "A Political Theory of Populism." *The Quarterly Journal of Economics* 128 (2): 771–805.

Akkerman, Agnes, Cas Mudde, and Andrej Zaslove. 2014. "How Populist Are the People? Measuring Populist Attitudes in Voters." *Comparative Political Studies* 47 (9): 1324–53.

Akkerman, Agnes, Andrej Zaslove, and Bram Spruyt. 2017. "'We the People' or 'We the Peoples'? A Comparison of Support for the Populist Radical Right and Populist Radical Left in the Netherlands." *Swiss Political Science Review* 23 (4): 377–403.

Andreadis, Ioannis, Kirk A. Hawkins, Cristóbal Rovira Kaltwasser, and Matthew M. Singer. 2019. "The Conditional Effects of Populist Attitudes on Voter Choices in Four Democracies." In *The Ideational Approach to Populism: Concept, Theory, and Analysis*, edited by Kirk A. Hawkins, Ryan Carlin, Levente Littvay, and Cristóbal Rovira Kaltwasser. London: Routledge.

Andreadis, Ioannis, and Saskia Pauline Ruth. 2019. "Elite Surveys." In *The Ideational Approach to Populism: Concept, Theory, and Analysis*, edited by Kirk A. Hawkins, Ryan Carlin, Levente Littvay, and Cristóbal Rovira Kaltwasser. London: Routledge.

Arceneaux, Kevin, and Stephen P. Nicholson. 2012. "Who Wants to Have a Tea Party? The Who, What, and Why of the Tea Party Movement." *PS Political Science and Politics* 45 (4): 700–10.

Armony, Ariel C., and Victor Armony. 2005. "Indictments, Myths, and Citizen Mobilization in Argentina: A Discourse Analysis." *Latin American Politics and Society* 47 (4): 27–54.

Aslanidis, Paris. 2016. "Is Populism an Ideology? A Refutation and a New Perspective." *Political Studies* 64 (1): 88–104.

Axelrod, Robert. 1967. "The Structure of Public Opinion on Policy Issues." *Public Opinion Quarterly* 31 (1): 51–60.

Barr, Rob. 2016. "Has Latin American Populism Spread to the US?" *Mobilizing Ideas* (blog). April 8, 2016. https://mobilizingideas.wordpress.com/2016/04/08/has-latin-american-populism-spread-to-the-us/.

Barr, Robert R. 2009. "Populists, Outsiders and Anti-Establishment Politics." *Party Politics* 15 (1): 29–48.

Batson, C. Daniel, and Nadia Y. Ahmad. 2009. "Using Empathy to Improve Intergroup Attitudes and Relations." *Social Issues and Policy Review* 3 (1): 141–77.

Berman, Sheri. 2017. "Populism Is a Problem. Elitist Technocrats Aren't the Solution." *Foreign Policy* (blog). December 20, 2017. https://foreignpolicy.com/2017/12/20/populism-is-a-problem-elitist-technocrats-arent-the-solution/.

Betz, Hans-Georg. 1994. *Radical Right-Wing Populism in Western Europe*. New York: St. Martins Press.

Bimes, Terri, and Quinn Mulroy. 2004. "The Rise and Decline of Presidential Populism." *Studies in American Political Development* 18 (2): 136–59.

Bonikowski, Bart, and Noam Gidron. 2016. "The Populist Style in American Politics: Presidential Campaign Discourse, 1952–1996." *Social Forces* 94 (4): 1593–621.

Bornschier, Simon. 2017. "Populist Mobilization Across Time and Space: An Introduction." *Swiss Political Science Review* 23 (4): 301–12.

Bos, Linda, Wouter Van Der Brug, and Claes H. De Vreese. 2013. "An Experimental Test of the Impact of Style and Rhetoric on the Perception of Right-Wing Populist and Mainstream Party Leaders." *Acta Politica* 48 (2): 192–208.

Bozóki, András, and Dániel Hegedűs. 2018. "An Externally Constrained Hybrid Regime: Hungary in the European Union." *Democratization* 25 (7): 1173–89.

Browning, Christopher R. 2018. "The Suffocation of Democracy." *The New York Review of Books*, October 25, 2018. www.nybooks.com/articles/2018/10/25/suffocation-of-democracy/.

Busby, Ethan, David Doyle, Kirk Hawkins, and Nina Wiesehomeier. 2019. "Activating Populist Attitudes: The Role of Corruption." In *The Ideational Approach to Populism: Concept, Theory, and Analysis*, edited by Kirk A. Hawkins, Ryan Carlin, Levente Littvay, and Cristóbal Rovira Kaltwasser. London: Routledge.

Busby, Ethan, Joshua Gubler, and Kirk Hawkins. 2019. "Framing and Blame Attribution in Populist Rhetoric." *Journal of Politics* 81 (2): 616–30.

Bright Line Watch. 2018. "Reports: Wave 4." February 8, 2018. http://bright linewatch.org/wave4/.

Calamur, Krishnadev. 2016. "What Europe's Far Right Sees in Trump's Win." *The Atlantic*, November 10, 2016. www.theatlantic.com/international/ archive/2016/11/trump-far-right-europe/507314/.

Canovan, Margaret. 1981. *Populism*. New York: Harcourt Brace Jovanovich.

1999. "Trust the People! Populism and the Two Faces of Democracy." *Political Studies* 47 (1): 2–16.

Caramani, Daniele. 2017. "Will vs. Reason: The Populist and Technocratic Forms of Political Representation and Their Critique to Party Government." *American Political Science Review* 111 (1): 54–67.

Cardoso, Fernando Henrique, and Enzo Faletto. 1979. *Dependency and Development in Latin America*. Berkeley: University of California Press.

Carroll, Rory. 2016. "Insult, Provoke, Repeat: How Donald Trump Became America's Hugo Chávez." *The Guardian*, June 22, 2016, sec. US news. www .theguardian.com/us-news/2016/jun/22/donald-trump-hugo-chavez-politi cal-similarities.

Chong, Dennis, and James N. Druckman. 2007. "Framing Theory." *Annual Review of Political Science* 10 (1): 103–26.

Cillizza, Chris. 2015. "Ben Carson Is the Least Understood Presidential Candidate. That's Good for Him." *Washington Post*, October 23, 2015, sec. The Fix. www.washingtonpost.com/news/the-fix/wp/2015/10/23/lots-of-peo ple-think-ben-carson-is-crazy-except-the-people-who-will-choose-the-gop-nominee/.

Colgan, Jeff D., and Robert O. Keohane. 2017. "The Liberal Order Is Rigged." *Foreign Affairs*, April 17, 2017.

Conniff, Michael L, ed. 1999. *Populism in Latin America*. Tuscaloosa: University of Alabama Press.

Cooperative Study of Electoral Systems. 2016. "CSES Announcement: The CSES Module 5 (2016–2021) Questionnaire Is Now Available." 2016. www .cses.org/announce/newsltr/20160930.htm.

Cramer, Katherine. 2016a. "Analysis | How Rural Resentment Helps Explain the Surprising Victory of Donald Trump." *Washington Post: Monkey Cage* (blog). November 13, 2016. www.washingtonpost.com/news/monkey-cage/ wp/2016/11/13/how-rural-resentment-helps-explain-the-surprising-victory-of-donald-trump/.

Cramer, Katherine J. 2016b. *The Politics of Resentment: Rural Consciousness in Wisconsin and the Rise of Scott Walker.* Chicago: University of Chicago Press.

Dai, Yaoyao. 2018. "Measuring Populism in Context: Introducing A Supervised Approach with Word Embedding Models." Paper presented at the Seventy-Sixth Annual MPSA Conference, April 5-8, Chicago.

Dai, Yaoyao, and Zijie Shao. 2016. "Populism and Authoritarian Survival in China: Concept and Measurement." *Comparative Politics Newsletter* 26 (2): 31–39.

Di Tella, Torcuato S. 1965. "Populism and Reform in Latin America." In *Obstacles to Change in Latin America,* edited by Claudio Véliz, 47–74. London: Oxford University Press.

Diamond, Larry. 2015. "Facing Up to the Democratic Recession." *Journal of Democracy* 26 (1): 141–55.

Dodd, Nigel, Michèle Lamont, and Mike Savage. 2017. "Introduction to BJS Special Issue." *The British Journal of Sociology* 68 (S1): 3–10.

Dornbusch, Rudiger, and Sebastian Edwards, eds. 1991. *The Macroeconomics of Populism in Latin America.* Chicago: University of Chicago Press.

Doyle, David. 2011. "The Legitimacy of Political Institutions Explaining Contemporary Populism in Latin America." *Comparative Political Studies* 44 (11): 1447–73.

Dryzek, John S., and Jeffrey Berejikian. 1993. "Reconstructive Democratic Theory." *American Political Science Review* 87 (1): 48–60.

Elchardus, Mark, and Bram Spruyt. 2016. "Populism, Persistent Republicanism and Declinism: An Empirical Analysis of Populism as a Thin Ideology." *Government and Opposition* 51 (1): 111–33.

Engesser, Sven, Nayla Fawzi, and Anders Olof Larsson. 2017. "Populist Online Communication: Introduction to the Special Issue." *Information, Communication and Society* 29 (9): 1279–92.

Fallend, Franz, and Reinhard Heinisch. 2016. "Collaboration as Successful Strategy against Right-Wing Populism? The Case of the Centre-Right Coalition in Austria, 2000–2007." *Democratization* 23 (2): 324–44.

Federal Reserve Bank of Atlanta. n.d. "Wage Growth Tracker." Accessed February 21, 2018. www.frbatlanta.org:443/chcs/wage-growth-tracker.

Feldman, Stanley. 2003. "Enforcing Social Conformity: A Theory of Authoritarianism." *Political Psychology* 24 (1): 41–74.

File, Thom. 2017. "Voting in America: A Look at the 2016 Presidential Election." The United States Census Bureau. May 10, 2017. www.census .gov/newsroom/blogs/random-samplings/2017/05/voting_in_america.html.

Fiorina, Morris P., Samuel A. Abrams, and Jeremy C. Pope. 2008. "Polarization in the American Public: Misconceptions and Misreadings." *The Journal of Politics* 70 (2): 556–60.

Foa, Roberto Stefan, and Yascha Mounk. 2017. "The Signs of Deconsolidation." Journal of Democracy 28 (1): 5–15.

Formisano, Ronald P. 2012. *The Tea Party: A Brief History.* Baltimore, MD: Johns Hopkins University Press.

Freeden, Michael. 2017. "After the Brexit Referendum: Revisiting Populism as an Ideology." *Journal of Political Ideologies* 22 (1): 1–11.

Galston, William A. 2018. *Anti-Pluralism: The Populist Threat to Liberal Democracy.* New Haven: Yale University Press.

Germani, Gino. 1978. *Authoritarianism, Fascism, and National Populism.* New Brunswick, NJ: Transaction Publishers.

Goodwyn, Lawrence. 1976. *Democratic Promise: The Populist Moment in America.* New York: Oxford University Press.

Grillo, Ioan. 2016. "Is Trump the U.S. Chávez?" *The New York Times,* November 3, 2016, sec. Opinion.

Gubler, Joshua Ronald, Eran Halperin, and Gilad Hirschberger. 2015. "Humanizing the Outgroup in Contexts of Protracted Intergroup Conflict." *Journal of Experimental Political Science* 2 (1): 36–46.

Hadiz, Vedi R, and Angelos Chryssogelos. 2017. "Populism in World Politics: A Comparative Cross-Regional Perspective." *International Political Science Review* 38 (4): 399–411.

Hameleers, Michael, Linda Bos, and Claes H. de Vreese. 2016. "'They Did It': The Effects of Emotionalized Blame Attribution in Populist Communication." *Communication Research* 44 (6): 870–900.

Handlin, Samuel. 2017. *State Crisis in Fragile Democracies: Polarization and Political Regimes in South America.* Cambridge: Cambridge University Press.

———. 2018. "The Logic of Polarizing Populism: State Crises and Polarization in South America." *American Behavioral Scientist* 62 (1): 75–91.

Hawkins, Kirk A. 2009. "Is Chávez Populist? Measuring Populist Discourse in Comparative Perspective." *Comparative Political Studies* 42 (8): 1040–67.

———. 2010. *Venezuela's Chavismo and Populism in Comparative Perspective.* Cambridge: Cambridge University Press.

———. 2016a. "Populism and the 2016 US Presidential Election in Comparative Perspective." *Comparative Politics Newsletter*, 2016.

———. 2016b. "Responding to Radical Populism: Chavismo in Venezuela." *Democratization* 23 (2): 242–62.

Hawkins, Kirk A., and Bruno Castanho Silva. 2019. "Textual Analysis: Big Data Approaches." In *The Ideational Approach to Populism: Concept,*

Theory, and Analysis, edited by Kirk A. Hawkins, Ryan Carlin, Levente Littvay, and Cristóbal Rovira Kaltwasser. London: Routledge.

Hawkins, Kirk A., Madeleine Read, and Teun Pauwels. 2017. "Populism and Its Causes." In *The Oxford Handbook of Populism*, edited by Cristobal Rovira Kaltwasser, Paul A. Taggart, Paulina Ochoa Espejo, and Pierre Ostiguy, 267–86. Oxford: Oxford University Press.

Hawkins, Kirk A., Scott Riding, and Cas Mudde. 2012. "Measuring Populist Attitudes." *Working Paper Series on Political Concepts, ECPR Committee on Concepts and Methods*. www.concepts-methods.org/Files/WorkingPaper/PC_55_Hawkins_Riding_Mudde.pdf.

Hawkins, Kirk A., and Cristóbal Rovira Kaltwasser. 2018. "Measuring Populist Discourse in the United States and Beyond." *Nature Human Behaviour* 2 (4): 241.

Hawkins, Kirk A., and Cristóbal Rovira Kaltwasser. 2019. "The Ideational Approach." In *The Ideational Approach to Populism: Concept, Theory, and Analysis*, edited by Kirk A. Hawkins, Ryan Carlin, Levente Littvay, and Cristóbal Rovira Kaltwasser. London: Routledge. 2017. "The Ideational Approach to Populism." *Latin American Research Review* 52 (3).

Hawkins, Kirk A., Cristobal Rovira Kaltwasser, and Ioannis Andreadis. 2018. "The Activation of Populist Attitudes." *Democracy and Opposition*. Online. https://doi.org/10.1017/gov.2018.23

Heer, Jeet. 2016. "Trump's Populism Is a Sham." *The New Republic*, December 9, 2016. https://newrepublic.com/article/139239/trumps-populism-sham.

Heinrich, Finn. 2017. "Corruption and Inequality: How Populists Mislead People." Transparency International. January 25, 2017. www.transparency.org/news/feature/corruption_and_inequality_how_populists_mislead_people.

Hetherington, Marc J., and Jonathan D. Weiler. 2009. *Authoritarianism and Polarization in American Politics*. Cambridge: Cambridge University Press.

Hibbing, John R., and Elizabeth Theiss-Morse. 2002. *Stealth Democracy: Americans' Beliefs About How Government Should Work*. Cambridge: Cambridge University Press.

Hofstadter, Richard. 1960. *The Age of Reform*. New York: Vintage Books.

Hooghe, Marc, and Ruth Dassonneville. 2018. "Explaining the Trump Vote: The Effect of Racist Resentment and Anti-Immigrant Sentiments." *PS: Political Science & Politics* online first (April): 1–7.

Houle, Christian, and Paul Kenny. 2018. "The Political and Economic Consequences of Populist Rule in Latin America." *Government and Opposition* 53 (2): 256–87.

Huber, Robert A., and Saskia P. Ruth. 2017. "Mind the Gap! Populism, Participation and Representation in Europe." *Swiss Political Science Review* 23 (4): 462–84.

Huber, Robert A., and Christian H. Schimpf. 2016. "Friend or Foe? Testing the Influence of Populism on Democratic Quality in Latin America." *Political Studies* 64 (4): 872–89.

Ianni, Octávio. 1975. *La formación del Estado populista en América Latina.* Mexico, D.F.: Ediciones Era.

Illing, Sean. 2017. "Trump Ran as a Populist. He's Governing as an Elitist. He's Not the First." Vox. June 23, 2017. www.vox.com/2017/6/23/15791432/donald-trump-populism-latin-america-republican-party.

Inglehart, Ronald, and Pippa Norris. 2016. "Trump, Brexit, and the Rise of Populism: Economic Have-Nots and Cultural Backlash." HKS Faculty Research Working Paper Series RWP16-026, August.

2017. "Trump and the Populist Authoritarian Parties: The Silent Revolution in Reverse." *Perspectives on Politics* 15 (2): 443–54.

Iyengar, Shanto, and Masha Krupenkin. 2018. "The Strengthening of Partisan Affect." *Political Psychology* 39 (S1): 201–18.

Iyengar, Shanto, Gaurav Sood, and Yphtach Lelkes. 2012. "Affect, Not Ideology: A Social Identity Perspective on Polarization." *Public Opinion Quarterly* 76 (3): 405–31.

Iyengar, Shanto, and Sean J. Westwood. 2015. "Fear and Loathing across Party Lines: New Evidence on Group Polarization." *American Journal of Political Science* 59 (3): 690–707.

Jacobson, Gary C. 2017. "The Triumph of Polarized Partisanship in 2016: Donald Trump's Improbable Victory." *Political Science Quarterly* 132 (1): 9–42.

Jagers, Jan, and Stefaan Walgrave. 2007. "Populism as Political Communication Style: An Empirical Study of Political Parties' Discourse in Belgium." *European Journal of Political Research* 46 (3): 319–45.

Johnston, David Cay. 2016. "Why Voters Elected President Donald J. Trump—and Why They'll Regret It." *The Daily Beast*, November 9, 2016. www.thedailybeast.com/articles/2016/11/09/why-voters-elected-president-donald-j-trump-and-why-they-ll-regret-it.

Judis, John B. 2016. *The Populist Explosion: How the Great Recession Transformed American and European Politics.* New York: Columbia Global Reports.

Karpowitz, Christopher F., J. Quin Monson, Kelly D. Patterson, and Jeremy C. Pope. 2011. "Tea Time in America? The Impact of the Tea Party Movement on the 2010 Midterm Elections." *PS: Political Science & Politics* 44 (02): 303 09.

Kazin, Michael. 1998. *The Populist Persuasion: An American History.* Ithaca, NY: Cornell University Press.

2016. "How Can Donald Trump and Bernie Sanders Both Be 'Populist'?" *The New York Times*, March 22, 2016. www.nytimes.com/2016/03/27/maga zine/how-can-donald-trump-and-bernie-sanders-both-be-populist.html.

Kenny, Paul. 2017. *Populism and Patronage: Why Populists Win Elections in India, Asia, and Beyond.* Oxford: Oxford University Press.

Kessel, Stijn van. 2015. *Populist Parties in Europe: Agents of Discontent?* New York: Palgrave Macmillan.

Kitschelt, Herbert. 1997. *The Radical Right in Western Europe: A Comparative Analysis.* Ann Arbor: University of Michigan Press.

Kornblith, Miriam. 2005. "Elections versus Democracy." *Journal of Democracy* 16 (1): 124–37.

Laclau, Ernesto. 1977. *Politics and Ideology in Marxist Theory: Capitalism, Fascism, Populism.* London: New Left Books.

Laclau, Ernesto. 2005. *On Populist Reason.* London: Verso Books.

Lamont, Michèle, Bo Yun Park, and Elena Ayala-Hurtado. 2017. "Trump's Electoral Speeches and His Appeal to the American White Working Class." *The British Journal of Sociology* 68 (S1): 154–80.

Latimer, Matt. 2015. "Seven Reasons the GOP Should Fear Donald Trump." POLITICO Magazine. June 16, 2015. www.politico.com/magazine/story/ 2015/06/donald-trump-2016-seven-reasons-to-fear-119069.html.

Levitsky, Steven, and Daniel Ziblatt. 2018. *How Democracies Die.* New York: Crown.

Levitsky, Steven, and James Loxton. 2013. "Populism and Competitive Authoritarianism in the Andes." *Democratization* 20 (1): 107–36.

Lowndes, Joseph. 2017. "Populism in the United States." In *The Oxford Handbook of Populism*, edited by Cristóbal Rovira Kaltwasser, Paul Taggart, Paulina Ochoa Espejo, and Pierre Ostiguy, 232–47. Oxford: Oxford University Press.

Mair, Peter. 2011. "Bini Smaghi vs. the Parties: Representative Government and Institutional Constraints." EUI Working Papers 2011/22. Robert Schuman Centre for Advanced Studies, European Union Democracy Observatory. http://hdl.handle.net/1814/16354.

Martinelli, Alberto, ed. 2017. *Beyond Trump: Populism on the Rise.* Milan: Edizioni Epoké.

Mascaro, Lisa. 2017. "Trump Speechwriter Stephen Miller, a Santa Monica High Grad, Pens Address for President's Middle East Visit." *Los Angeles*

Times, May 19, 2017. www.latimes.com/politics/washington/la-na-essential-washington-updates-trump-speechwriter-stephen-miller-pens-1495224315-htmlstory.html.

Matthes, Jörg, and Desirée Schmuck. 2017. "The Effects of Anti-Immigrant Right-Wing Populist Ads on Implicit and Explicit Attitudes: A Moderated Mediation Model." *Communication Research* 44 (4): 556–81.

McCann, Stewart J. H. 2009. "Political Conservatism, Authoritarianism, and Societal Threat: Voting for Republican Representatives in U.S. Congressional Elections From 1946 to 1992." *The Journal of Psychology* 143 (4): 341–58.

McClosky, Herbert, and Dennis Chong. 1985. "Similarities and Differences Between Left-Wing and Right-Wing Radicals." *British Journal of Political Science* 15 (3): 329–63.

McCoy, Jennifer, and Francisco Diez. 2011. *International Mediation in Venezuela*. Washington, DC: US Institute of Peace Press.

McCoy, Jennifer, Tahmina Rahman, and Murat Somer. 2018. "Polarization and the Global Crisis of Democracy: Common Patterns, Dynamics, and Pernicious Consequences for Democratic Polities." *American Behavioral Scientist* 62 (1): 16–42.

Mechkova, Valeriya, Anna Lührmann, and Staffan I. Lindberg. 2017. "How Much Democratic Backsliding?" *Journal of Democracy* 28 (4): 162–69.

Medzihorsky, Juraj, Levente Littvay, and Erin K. Jenne. 2014. "Has the Tea Party Era Radicalized the Republican Party? Evidence from Text Analysis of the 2008 and 2012 Republican Primary Debates." *PS: Political Science & Politics* 47 (04): 806–12.

Mickey, Robert. 2017. "Anti-Anti Populism, or: The Threat of Populism to U.S. Democracy Is Exaggerated." In *Global Populisms: A Threat to Democracy?* Stanford, CA: Freeman Spogli Institution for International Studies. https://fsi-live.s3.us-west-1.amazonaws.com/s3fs-public/rob_mickey.pdf.

Moffitt, Benjamin. 2016. *The Global Rise of Populism: Performance, Political Style, and Representation*. Palo Alto, CA: Stanford University Press.

Mondak, Jeffery J., Matthew V. Hibbing, Damarys Canache, Mitchell A. Seligson, and Mary R. Anderson. 2010. "Personality and Civic Engagement: An Integrative Framework for the Study of Trait Effects on Political Behavior." *American Political Science Review* 104 (01): 85–110.

Mudde, Cas. 2004. "The Populist Zeitgeist." *Government and Opposition* 39 (4): 542–63.

2007. *Populist Radical Right Parties in Europe*. Cambridge: Cambridge University Press.

2015. "The Trump Phenomenon and the European Populist Radical Right." *The Washington Post* (blog). August 26, 2015. www.washingtonpost.com/ blogs/monkey-cage/wp/2015/08/26/the-trump-phenomenon-and-the-eur opean-populist-radical-right/.

Mudde, Cas, and Cristóbal Rovira Kaltwasser. 2018. "Studying Populism in Comparative Perspective: Reflections on the Contemporary and Future Research Agenda." *Comparative Political Studies.* 51 (13): 1667–1693.

Mudde, Cas, and Cristobal Rovira Kaltwasser, eds. 2012. *Populism in Europe and the Americas: Threat or Corrective to Democracy?* Cambridge: Cambridge University Press.

Mudde, Cas, and Cristóbal Rovira Kaltwasser. 2013a. "Exclusionary vs. Inclusionary Populism: Comparing Contemporary Europe and Latin America." *Government and Opposition* 48 (2): 1–28.

2013b. "Exclusionary vs. Inclusionary Populism: Comparing Contemporary Europe and Latin America." *Government and Opposition* 48 (02): 147–74. https://doi.org/10.1017/gov.2012.11.

2017. *Populism: A Very Short Introduction.* Oxford: Oxford University Press.

Muller, Jan-Werner. 2016. *What Is Populism?* Philadelphia: University of Pennsylvania Press.

Nelson, Thomas E., Zoe M. Oxley, and Rosalee A. Clawson. 1997. "Toward a Psychology of Framing Effects." *Political Behavior* 19 (3): 221–46.

Espejo, Paulina Ochoa. 2011. *The Time of Popular Sovereignty: Process and the Democratic State.* University Park: Penn State Press.

Oliver, Eric J., and Wendy M. Rahn. 2016. "The Rise of the Trumpenvolk: Populism in the 2016 Election." *Annals of the American Academy of Political and Social Sciences* 667 (1).

Packer, George. 2015. "The Pros and Cons of Populism." *The New Yorker,* August 30, 2015. www.newyorker.com/magazine/2015/09/07/the-populists.

Panizza, Francisco, ed. 2005. *Populism and the Mirror of Democracy.* London: Verso Books.

Parker, Christopher S., and Matt A. Barreto. 2013. *Change They Can't Believe In: The Tea Party and Reactionary Politics in America.* Princeton, NJ: Princeton University Press.

Pauwels, Teun. 2014. *Populism in Western Europe: Comparing Belgium, Germany and The Netherlands.* New York: Routledge.

Phillips, Amber. 2015. "5 Times Ted Cruz Went to War with the Republican Establishment." *Washington Post,* December 22, 2015, sec. The Fix. www .washingtonpost.com/news/the-fix/wp/2015/12/22/5-times-ted-cruz-went-to-war-with-the-republican-establishment/.

Plattner, Marc F. 2010. "Populism, Pluralism, and Liberal Democracy." *Journal of Democracy* 21 (1): 81–92.

Polk, Jonathan, Jan Rovny, Ryan Bakker, Erica Edwards, Liesbet Hooghe, Seth Jolly, Jelle Koedam, Filip Kostelka, Gary Marks, and Gijs Schumacher. 2017. "Explaining the Salience of Anti-Elitism and Reducing Political Corruption for Political Parties in Europe with the 2014 Chapel Hill Expert Survey Data." *Research & Politics* 4 (1): 1–9.

Rahn, Wendy. 2019. "The Making of a Populist Moment: The 2016 US Election in Context." In *The Ideational Approach to Populism: Concept, Theory, and Analysis*, edited by Kirk A. Hawkins, Ryan Carlin, Levente Littvay, and Cristóbal Rovira Kaltwasser. London: Routledge.

Rasmussen, Scott, and Doug Schoen. 2010. *Mad As Hell: How the Tea Party Movement Is Fundamentally Remaking Our Two-Party System*. New York: Harper.

Rico, Guillem, Marc Guinjoan, and Eva Anduiza. 2017. "The Emotional Underpinnings of Populism: How Anger and Fear Affect Populist Attitudes." *Swiss Political Science Review* 23 (4): 444–61.

Roberts, Kenneth M. 1995. "Neoliberalism and the Transformation of Populism in Latin America: The Peruvian Case." *World Politics* 48 (01): 82–116.

Rodrik, Dani. 2017. "Populism and the Economics of Globalization." Working Paper 23559. National Bureau of Economic Research. https://doi.org/10.3386/w23559.

Rooduijn, Matthijs, Wouter van der Brug, and Sarah L. de Lange. 2016. "Expressing or Fuelling Discontent? The Relationship between Populist Voting and Political Discontent." *Electoral Studies* 43 (September): 32–40.

Rooduijn, Matthijs, and Teun Pauwels. 2011. "Measuring Populism: Comparing Two Methods of Content Analysis." *West European Politics* 34 (6): 1272–83.

Rosas, Guillermo, Noel P. Johnston, and Kirk Hawkins. 2014. "Local Public Goods as Vote-Purchasing Devices? Persuasion and Mobilization in the Choice of Clientelist Payments." *Journal of Theoretical Politics* 26 (4): 573–98.

Rovira Kaltwasser, Cristóbal, and Paul Taggart. 2016. "Dealing with Populists in Government: A Framework for Analysis." *Democratization* 23 (2): 201–20. https://doi.org/10.1080/13510347.2015.1058785.

Rovira Kaltwasser, Cristóbal, Paul Taggart, Paulina Ochoa Espejo, and Pierre Ostiguy. 2017. "Populism: An Overview of the Concept and the State of the Art." In *The Oxford Handbook of Populism*, edited by Cristóbal Rovira Kaltwasser, Paul Taggart, Paulina Ochoa Espejo, and Pierre Ostiguy, 1–24. Oxford: Oxford University Press.

Sachs, Jeffrey D. 1989. "Social Conflict and Populist Policies in Latin America." Working Paper 2897. NBER Working Paper. Cambridge, MA: National Bureau of Economic Research. https://doi.org/10.3386/w2897.

Schaffner, Brian F., Matthew Macwilliams, and Tatishe Nteta. 2018. "Understanding White Polarization in the 2018 Vote for President: The Sobering Role of Racism and Sexism." *Political Science Quarterly* 133 (1): 9–34.

Schulz, Anne, Philipp Müller, Christian Schemer, Dominique Stefanie Wirz, Martin Wettstein, and Werner Wirth. 2018. "Measuring Populist Attitudes on Three Dimensions." *International Journal of Public Opinion Research* 30 (2): 316–26.

Sides, John, and Michael Tesler. 2016. "How Political Science Helps Explain the Rise of Trump (part 3): It's the Economy, Stupid." *Washington Post*. May 4, 2016. www.washingtonpost.com/news/monkey-cage/wp/2016/03/04/how-political-science-helps-explain-the-rise-of-trump-part-3-its-the-economy-stupid/.

Sides, John, Michael Tesler, and Lynn Vavreck. 2017. "How Trump Lost and Won." *Journal of Democracy* 28 (2): 34–44.

2018. "Hunting Where the Ducks Are: Activating Support for Donald Trump in the 2016 Republican Primary." *Journal of Elections, Public Opinion and Parties* 28 (2): 135–56.

Silva, Bruno Castanho, Erin K. Jenne, Nebojša Blanuša, and Levente Littvay. 2018. "The Psychological Underpinnings of Populist Attitudes." Paper presented at the Research Workshop "Populist Attitudes in Comparative Perspective," Bamberg, Germany, 13 June.

Silva, Bruno Castanho. 2019. "Populist Success: A Qualitative Comparative Analysis." In *The Ideational Approach to Populism: Concept, Theory, and Analysis*, edited by Kirk A. Hawkins, Ryan Carlin, Levente Littvay, and Cristóbal Rovira Kaltwasser. London: Routledge.

Silva, Bruno Castanho, Ioannis Andreadis, Eva Anduiza, Nebojša Blanuša, Yazmin Morlet Corti, Gisela Delfino, Guillem Rico, et al. 2019. "Public Opinion Surveys: A New Scale." In *The Ideational Approach to Populism: Concept, Theory, and Analysis*, edited by Kirk A. Hawkins, Ryan Carlin, Levente Littvay, and Cristóbal Rovira Kaltwasser. London: Routledge.

Silva, Bruno Castanho, Federico Vegetti, and Levente Littvay. 2017. "The Elite Is up to Something: Exploring the Relation between Populism and Belief in Conspiracy Theories." *Swiss Political Science Review* 23 (4): 423–43.

Skocpol, Theda, and Vanessa Williamson. 2013. *The Tea Party and the Remaking of Republican Conservatism*. Reprint edition. New York: Oxford University Press.

Spruyt, Bram, Gil Keppens, and Filip Van Droogenbroek. 2016. "Who Supports Populism and What Attracts People to It?" *Political Research Quarterly* 69 (2): 335–46.

Stanley, Ben. 2016. "Confrontation by Default and Confrontation by Design: Strategic and Institutional Responses to Poland's Populist Coalition Government." *Democratization* 23 (2): 263–82.

Stenner, Karen. 2005. *The Authoritarian Dynamic*. Cambridge: Cambridge University Press.

Stone, Walter J., and Ronald Rapoport. 2008. *Three's a Crowd: The Dynamic of Third Parties, Ross Perot, and Republican Resurgence*. Ann Arbor: University of Michigan Press.

Sudweeks, R. R., S. Reeve, and W. S. Bradshaw. 2004. "A Comparison of Generalizability Theory and Many-Facet Rasch Measurement in an Analysis of College Sophomore Writing." *Assessing Writing* 9 (3): 239–61.

The Economist. 2017. "Populism in America: The Future of Bannonism." *The Economist*, August 29, 2017.

The Telegraph. 2015. "The Trump Manifesto." *The Telegraph*, June 17, 2015. www.telegraph.co.uk/news/worldnews/us-election/11679626/The-Trump-manifesto.html.

The World Bank. n.d. "GDP Growth (Annual %)." Accessed February 21, 2018. https://data.worldbank.org/indicator/NY.GDP.MKTP.KD.ZG.

de la Torre, Carlos. 2000. *Populist Seduction in Latin America: The Ecuadorian Experience*. Athens, Ohio: Ohio University Press.

de la Torre, Carlos, and Andrés Ortiz. 2015. "Populist Polarization and the Slow Death of Democracy in Ecuador." *Democratization*. https://doi.org/10.1080/13510347.2015.1058784.

Transparency International. n.d. "Corruption Perceptions Index 2016." Accessed February 21, 2018. www.transparency.org/news/feature/corruption_perceptions_index_2016.

Urbinati, Nadia. 1998. "Democracy and Populism." *Constellations* 5 (1): 110–24.

US Department of Labor. n.d. "Bureau of Labor Statistics Data." Accessed February 21, 2018. https://data.bls.gov/timeseries/LNS14000000.

Van Hauwaert, Steven, and Stijn van Kessel. 2018. "Beyond Protest and Discontent: A Cross-national Analysis of the Effect of Populist Attitudes and Issue Positions on Populist Party Support." *European Journal of Political Research* 57 (1): 68–92.

Van Hauwaert, Steven M., Christian H. Schimpf, and Flavio Azevedo. 2019. "Evaluating Existing Survey Measures of Demand-Side Populism Using IRT." In *The Ideational Approach to Populism: Concept, Theory, and*

Analysis, edited by Kirk A. Hawkins, Ryan Carlin, Levente Littvay, and Cristóbal Rovira Kaltwasser. London: Routledge.

Voss, McKinney. 2018. "The Populism of Andrew Jackson: Memorandum." Team Populism. April 23, 2018. https://populism.byu.edu/Pages/Data.

Weffort, Francisco C. 1978. *O Populismo Na Política Brasileira*. Coleção Estudos Brasileiros; v. 25. Rio de Janeiro: Paz e Terra.

Weyland, Kurt. 1999. "Neoliberal Populism in Latin America and Eastern Europe." *Comparative Politics* 31 (4): 379–401.

2001. "Clarifying a Contested Concept: Populism in the Study of Latin American Politics." *Comparative Politics* 34 (1): 1–22.

Weyland, Kurt, and Raúl L. Madrid. 2017. "Liberal Democracy Is Stronger Than Trump's Populism." *The American Interest*, December 11, 2017.

White, Edward M. 1985. *Teaching and Assessing Writing: Recent Advances in Understanding, Evaluating, and Improving Student Performance*. San Francisco: Jossey-Bass Publishers.

Wiesehomeier, Nina. 2019. "Expert Surveys." In *The Ideational Approach to Populism: Concept, Theory, and Analysis*, edited by Kirk A. Hawkins, Ryan Carlin, Levente Littvay, and Cristóbal Rovira Kaltwasser. London: Routledge.

Williamson, Kevin D. 2015. "The Art of the Con, by Donald Trump." *The National Review*. June 21, 2015. www.nationalreview.com/2015/06/donald-trump-puts-camp-campaign/.

Wodak, Ruth, and Michał Krzyżanowski. 2017. "Right-Wing Populism in Europe & USA." *Journal of Language and Politics* 16 (4): 471–84.

World Bank, Worth. 1997. *Helping Countries Combat Corruption: The Role of the World Bank*. Washington, DC: World Bank.

Acknowledgments

We would like to thank Erin Jenne and Rosario Aguilar (Bush and Obama speech data and endless support), Bruno Castanho Silva (for things too long to list in 30,000 words), Martin Mölder (figures), Caner Şimşek (on Turkey), Steven Van Hauwaert (for helping us navigate his appendices and replication materials for survey data comparisons), Rebecca Dudley (finding and coding speeches), Bojana Kocijan (managing coders), Cristóbal Sandoval (coding speeches), Fred Wen Jie Tan (finding speeches and managing data), McKinney Voss (a little of everything), and other friends of Team Populism (coding and advice). Team Populism is a cross-regional scholarly network dedicated to the study of populism's causes and consequences. Many of the ideas in this book reflect the efforts and insights of this network, and some of our colleagues are coauthors of individual sections. We also thank the BYU Department of Political Science and College of Family, Home, and Social Sciences for funding the coding, surveys, and an author's conference; Central European University for the Intellectual Themes Initiative funding of the Comparative Populism Project; and Cristóbal Rovira Kaltwasser for funding part of the coding. A very special shout-out goes to the Cambridge University Press Elements team for their patience and support, especially to the series editor Frances Lee and to senior content manager Joshua Penney.

This Element is dedicated to Andrew, Edward, Lucy, Henry, Johanna and Félix.

Cambridge Elements ⹋

American Politics

Elements in the Series

A full series listing is available at: www.cambridge.org/core/series/elements-in-
american-politics

Printed in the United States
By Bookmasters